also by nevada barr

Flashback

Hunting Season

Blood Lure

Deep South

Liberty Falling

Blind Descent

Endangered Species

Firestorm

Ill Wind

A Superior Death

Track of the Cat

Bittersweet

G. P. Putnam's Sons
New York
2003

seeking enlightenment... hat by hat

a skeptic's path to religion

nevada barr

G. P. Putnam's Sons
Publishers Since 1838
a member of
Penguin Group (USA) Inc.
375 Hudson Street
New York, NY 10014

Published simultaneously in Canada

Library of Congress Cataloging-in-Publication Data

Barr, Nevada.
Seeking enlightenment . . . hat by hat / Nevada Barr.
p. cm.
ISBN 0-399-15057-9
1. Barr, Nevada. 2. Novelists, American—20th century—
Biography. 3. Barr, Nevada—Religion. 4. Spiritual life. I. Title.
PS3552.A73184Z464 2003 2003043101
813'.54—dc21

Printed in the United States of America
1 3 5 7 9 10 8 6 4 2

This book is printed on acid-free paper. ♾

Book design by Stephanie Huntwork

For Molly and Mari, Sharon, Debra, Debbe, Joan, Bobbi, Linda,
Marty, Barbara, Sylvia, for Polly and Martha, for all the
women with whom I've talked and cried and talked
and had marvelous times discovering
the pathways of our lives.

contents

seeking enlightenment...
hat by hat

introduction

In Mississippi, where I now live, people still talk about God in everyday conversation. When the name "Jesus" pops up (and not in the context of taking names in vain), nobody squirms or rolls their eyes. One of the getting-to-know-you questions asked at picnics and bar-b-ques is: "What church do you go to?"

People not only talk about God, they talk *to* Him. And then they tell you about it. When I moved here, I was a godless heathen, and proud of it. According to the priest at the Episcopal church, I am still a heathen but no longer godless.

I doubt a trip to Dixie would bring God into everybody's life but, when I arrived, I had pretty much exhausted all other avenues. I'd failed me and, in the process, managed to screw up everything around me. My marriage had gone down in flames; I'd been rightly tossed out on my ear with little more than a suitcase full of paperback books and my clothes. I was clinically depressed, haunted by nightmares, broke, and, at forty-one, embarking on my third career, this time as a law-enforcement ranger for the National Park Service.

Now that I have weaseled my way back to life through grace, it seems to me that despair is one of the greatest sins. Even Judas probably would have been okay—maybe even become a model citizen—had he not despaired of being forgiven and hanged himself. I was as Judas; I despaired. It's entirely possible that I would have hanged myself had I not known my sister would kill me if I did such a thing. To wax poetic, with imagery fitting such a divine concept: I more or less ran into God at the bottom of the barrel.

At first, when I heard folks drawling the words "God" or, worse, "Jesus," I heard them through the double filter of misery as lonely and bleak as the Smoke Creek Desert in January and a background that scorned organized religion.

My upbringing provided no education on how to interact with the divine and no sense that God, if there were a god, which was suspect in itself, would deign to reside in people. With all the places to be when one is omnipresent, surely nothing less than a cat would do for Him. My family attended no churches, read no spiritual books and, by unspoken decree, the discussion of sex, religion, and politics was banned at our dinner table. Biblical terms were used exclusively for swearing. As oaths, they were moderately acceptable, certainly more so than scatological obscenities when it came to expressing strong emotion.

As an adult, from remembered scraps of conversations with my dad, I realized that my paternal grandmother had been the sort of Christian who used the Bible Belt to beat the fear of God into her children. It left Dad, and so his offspring, with a sour taste in their mouths when it came to naming the divine.

"God helps those who help themselves," was the extent of my belief system. And I helped myself to pretty much everything. Finally I helped myself right out of a marriage.

In my post-divorce months, between drinking too much and playing with sharp objects, I had a brief go at God. Cursing Him, screaming at Him, begging—the usual one-sided conversations of a very nearly terminally selfish person—but that was as far as any connection with a higher power evolved.

When Mississippians first started Jesusing and Godding right in front of me—and in broad daylight—I was most uncomfortable. I didn't quite know where to put my eyes or whether or not to laugh, sort of like when somebody tells a joke that you suspect might be in bad taste but aren't entirely sure. It made me nervous. When people talk to God, it makes everybody nervous. At least every Yankee. There's the creepy feeling that those who talk to God actually think He's listening; that they believe they've got an edge you lack.

It's worse in the South. Not only do people talk to God on a regular basis, but God talks to them and they tell you about it.

It's common to hear someone down here say, "I prayed about it and God told me to . . ." or, "I'm just waiting for a call from God before I decide what my college major's going to be."

I never got a call from God. Not a call, not a fax, not an e-mail, not a message in a bottle. My prayers positively echoed in the celestial silence. I occasionally heard voices—still do when it comes to that—but they were mere whispers, sentence fragments at the edges of my mind out of the dusk between sleep and waking. Surely not even the God of the shining countenance would choose to be as cryptic as my whispers. I didn't like it that He talked to everybody else. It made me twitchy to think they thought they were that right, that special. My voices, the mutterings in my mind, are fairly anonymous. Might be God, might be me. On a darker day, it might be Beelzebub. He's supposed to be a clever fellow.

Since God was out of the bag, socially speaking, here, I asked people how they knew, to quote Guy Clark, "if it was an angel or a ghost." I got no answers that satisfied. I asked how people came to be "called to God." The answers to this were less vague: handwriting on the wall of a room at the Comfort Inn, a direct intercession from St. Michael to change the outcome of a civil suit, a full-blown vision of the Virgin Mary on the front stoop of a home office, near-death experiences, a sense of Jesus coming into the heart.

I was not unduly disappointed to be out of the loop. Having God talk to me was not an idea I was all that crazy about. Sure, it would indicate He existed, but what if He decided to tell me to do something wretched like give away all my stuff and work with lepers in Guatemala? No, I did not particularly want to hear directly from any deity. I did envy the divine manifestations, however. How much could it cost Him to burn one lousy little bush for me?

I resented the fact that miracles were said to abound in the early days but no longer. The faithful are quick to tell you that miracles do happen, the miracle in a baby's smile and so forth. What a crock. They know precisely what we mean: real miracles, smoke and mirrors, sleight-of-hand, drop-your-jaw sorts of stuff. I've also been told: "You've got to have faith." To that, I say: Pshaw. If you already have faith, you don't need miracles. Old Testament magic was used to amaze the unbeliever. Whatever happened to that?

There's a great scene in *Shenandoah* where patriarch Jimmy Stewart says grace. He is not a religious man but has promised his dead wife he will teach the children the ways of the church. I can't remember it exactly, but the gist of it is: "Dear Lord, thank you for this food that is before us, food *we* grew and *we* harvested from land *we* cleared . . ." That's a grace I, or my father before me, might have given.

For all intents and purposes, I'd been my own god. Then, when I married, my husband and I made gods of one another. When these were toppled, I fell into a hell that mirrored the definition I'd once been given by a Sister of Mercy: an eternity locked away from the face of God.

After several years in the South, growing accustomed to hearing Christian words in a context other than blasphemy, I was no closer to enlightenment, but I'd come to suspect that *I* was not God. As it turned out, this was the first step in my spiritual rehabilitation. They say nature abhors a vacuum. Apparently God does, too. As long as my heart was filled with Me there was little room for anything else.

About this time, in a last-ditch effort to stop the pain caused by the divorce, my ex-husband and I embarked upon an ill-fated adventure we dubbed the Great Experiment. The idea was, after three years of disintegration and four years of separation, to get back together again. To this end I quit my job and moved myself, two cats, and a dog back to Durango, Colorado. This was more complicated than it sounds, but I'll spare you the details. You can get the general idea by watching any soap opera.

The tragic flaw in the plan was that my ex had quietly fallen in love with another woman several weeks before I loaded my life into a Beacon van and headed west.

My welcome was confusing, to say the least. I arrived anxious to begin the Great Experiment and instead ran into an emotional wall that I didn't understand.

Because pain without drama was unknown to me—part of the entitlement of my deeply held and never-examined beliefs was that each and every one of my emotions was worthy of a Busby Berkeley production—and because it was the Christmas season, a time when past joys become present aches, I went walking alone at dusk. Leather jacket, leather boots, slouch hat, Levis: I was a picture of . . . what? Perhaps Barbara Stanwyck in *The Big Valley,* a lone and lonely figure forging through the spitting snow and coming dark.

Small snug houses, strung with Christmas lights and glowing gold at the windows, helped me to feel outcast and uniquely miserable. Three blocks from my rented apartment I came to a church. Early winter night blackened the brick, and the low ceiling of drifting flakes made the edifice seem unnaturally tall. The gothic-inspired front was filled with a stained-glass window dimly lighted from within.

Though raised agnostic and become atheist in conversation if not in desperation, I stopped in the snow and gazed up at the window. I was drawn not by God but by Hollywood: Loretta Young in *The Bishop's Wife,* Ingrid Bergman in *The Bells of St. Mary's.* I would try the door, it would be locked, then, tragically, abandoned by God and Man, I would go to my lonely bed.

My plot was unexpectedly thickened; the doors were open. Inside were four women, seated not in the pews but on the carpet before the steps leading up to the altar. Most of the light came from candles, and there was a low, compelling drift of medieval choir song.

I would like to say the story continued in the seamless movie that I had been scripting in my subconscious, but such was not the case. No Cary Grant, no David Niven, no Bing Crosby: old dead Jesus hanging on the cross and four middle-aged women in snow boots.

It was just churchy as hell. I felt self-conscious, superior, intrusive, unwanted, and out of place. I turned to slink away. Those wily Christians were having none of that. The wretched creatures welcomed me, and I was suddenly stuck in a reality not of my own making.

They were engaged in a Taizé ceremony. I didn't know then what that was. Cross-legged on the rug we read words that meant little to me and listened to stunningly beautiful music from a tape played on a boom box balanced on the altar rail. At the end of the short ritual, a crude wooden cross three feet by two feet was laid on the steps. One by one the women laid hands on it and silently poured their pain into the forgiving hands of Jesus. When my turn came, I poured mine into dead wood. As soon as it was over, I made good my escape. Oddly, though, I felt better, lighter, but basically unchanged.

That Sunday I put on my good clothes and walked to the church. I found out it was St. Anthony's Episcopal. I knew Episcopalians were sort of watered-down Catholics, but that was the extent of my education. I had not seen the light; I had not been saved. My ex-husband, struggling with his own demons, had made the rule that we should see each other only once a week. I had no job, no friends. Church was just something to do, a reason to get dressed.

I was invited to Wednesday Bible Study class. There was a free meal and people to eat it with. I began to go. I felt a fake and a fraud, as if someone might leap up at any moment and denounce me as an unbeliever. But I was warm, fed, and with people. For that I was grateful enough to hold my tongue and be civil.

My sister came for the week between Christmas and New Year's. It was one of the many times in our long association that she chose to save me, if only temporarily, from whatever hell I'd made of my life this time. Her presence threw me into a dilemma. I wanted to continue to go to church. I don't know why. If I'd found meaning there, I couldn't articulate it. I just wanted to be present, to wear a nice dress and kneel. I especially felt the need to kneel. Since I'd not learned the art of prayer, I kneeled wordlessly, but the physical act made me feel better.

I couldn't tell my sister I'd started going to church—I didn't want to worry her. In our house, religion was seen as the opiate of the masses, a vehicle designed by the evil to fleece the gullible. Lord knows there is history to prove that theory if one chooses to look for it. Christians were at the bottom of a reviled list, often referred to by my father as "psalm-singing sons of bitches." I considered sneaking off to church and telling my sister I was going out to score drugs or meet a married man. Those activities would surely be less shocking than what I actually had in mind.

I was saved from having to come clean. The flu took care of my going anywhere for a couple of weeks, and my sister was safely back in California before the question of church arose again. Every Wednesday and Sunday I went. I listened and ate spaghetti off paper plates, I knelt and wondered what I was doing there.

In February, I went into a jewelry store and bought a cross, very tiny, on a thin gold chain. Like a teenager buying condoms, I told the jeweler it was for a friend. It was a needless lie and, as I told it, I found my need to do so most peculiar. I was embarrassed. I didn't want this stranger—who was happy simply to be making a sale—to think I was one of *them:* the gullible, the sanctimonious, the close-minded.

Why buy the damn thing then?

It was like the kneeling: I wanted to. I felt better near a cross even while ashamed to be seen wearing one. Back in the privacy of my apartment, I put the cross on and looked at myself in the mirror. It looked and felt distinctly alien and somehow dangerous next to my skin. I put on a turtleneck so nobody would see it.

That Wednesday Father Andrew showed us maps of Jesus' travels. The story of the savior was acted out on a chunk of land around eighty miles long and half that wide—about the size of that between my hometown of Susanville, California, and Reno, Nevada. The Holy Land was even more bleak and arid than the eastern slope of the Sierra. I knew what it was to walk in country like that. There was still no deep meaning to me, but blood started to flow into the men and women described in the stilted language of the gospels.

Because of the life I had led and the terrible price it had exacted, I was drawn to confession and penance. My first sincere prayer was: "I have sinned against you in thought, word, and deed, by what I have done and by what I have left undone." The concept of forgiveness made no sense to me. In my mind, forgiveness had two forms: indifference and condescension laced with resentment. Confession and penance I approached as if they were currency; enough of it and I could buy back the goodwill of those I had harmed. And, like the kneeling and the cross, it made me feel marginally better. Had hair shirts and self-flagellation been an option, I would have embraced them. Even the minor pain of listing my sins was a distraction from thoughts that cut me. My prayers were now sincere, but they were to a god made in my own image.

By March, I wished to be confirmed in the Episcopal church, though I knew I did not believe and I was not a Christian. I knelt and I wore the cross openly now, but I was not a Christian. I went to Father Andrew and told him this, told him I saw the lessons as metaphors, stories to help us work and play well with others. I told him I didn't believe, and I wanted to be confirmed. I asked if this was okay. He said it was.

I was grateful and suspicious. There was a touch of disappointment, too, a scattered illogical sense that if God were real, I shouldn't be allowed to be confirmed since I didn't believe. On some level, I wanted to be rejected, to have my views of Christians ratified even as I found comfort following their practices.

The Great Experiment ground to an ignoble close. I was out a bushel of dreams, a wagonload of hope, and a not inconsiderable amount of cash, but there was recompense: I had found an avenue along which I might travel in search of that "peace which passeth all understanding."

I returned to Mississippi and joined the Episcopal Church of the Creator near my home in Clinton. I go. I wear a nice dress. I kneel. And now I sing praises as well as lamentations, and my prayers of gratitude outnumber my confessions.

In the years since I have been on a wonderful spiritual journey, sometimes Christian, sometimes not, but always in community with other people—a state of being I avoided most of my life—and always with the grace of Sundays with music and the peculiar magic that can be found where a group gathers in His name—regardless of the name chosen to dignify the sense of something greater than ourselves.

This book is a collection of thoughts, meditations, failures, and successes that have come to me during this trip and, to quote Jerry Garcia, "What a long strange trip it's been." I've never been one to learn from the mistakes of others. For me, each and every pitfall must be tumbled into personally. Consequently, I cannot offer a neat map of how I traveled from an empty life to a life filled with joy. I cannot even offer the carrot of a life *consistently* filled with joy. I continue to chase after phantoms, go back on my word, screw up the best-laid plans, regress, digress, slip up, and fall off wagons of every stripe.

The motto of my alma mater, California Polytechnic State University in San Luis Obispo, California, was, "Learn by doing." Apparently I took it to heart.

Several years ago, my husband (not only did I find God in Mississippi, I found a *man*) and I went trekking in Nepal. We traveled with a tour group of eighteen other hikers. At the end of the trip, we spent three days in Chitwan National Park on the border between Nepal and India. The second day there a naturalist took us on a guided walk. He herded the group slowly through the jungle, pointing out the natural phenomena and explaining each in detail as our pod of humanity moved along. The last of these that I listened to was a dissertation on the track of a tiger found in the tall grasses—taller than a grown man—at the edge of the dirt road we followed.

As we clustered around this uninteresting bit of scuffed earth, something inside me snapped. Suddenly I needed to put space between myself and the people I had been jostling elbows with for the past ten days. Slipping away from the outer fringes of the pod, I began walking down the road that curled away out of sight in the primeval meadow we were crossing.

The naturalist, noticing my escape, began to yell: "Come back. Come back. Don't leave the group. Stay with the group."

Pretending not to hear, I kept walking. As I rounded the bend out of sight, I could hear him crying: "The tiger will eat you! The tiger will eat you!"

At that moment in time I didn't care if the tiger ate me. Better by far to be lunch for a tiger than to spend one more moment in the suffocating crush of the pod.

I have always insisted on my right to be eaten by the tiger, to risk myself to seek what calls me. I have fought against rules that sought to restrain me even when that restraint was for my own protection.

Sometimes the tiger ate me. The consequences of my acts cost me dearly, left scars. Sometimes the tiger let me alone.

This is a book about questing into the realms of the tigers emotionally, physically, and spiritually.

on getting into heaven

Having made my living much of my life by writing fiction, I know when I, or those around me, are making things up, when our plotlines drift free of the earth and we begin to weave tales of explanation, justification or—in most cases—tales of what we would *like* our story to be. We like stories where we are the star.

A whole lot of the ideologies I read focused on being the Chosen of God, the chosen—Us—and the not-chosen—those who are Not Us. This is rather like not being picked for a team in the third grade. To be among any given group of the

Chosen, one had to follow an intricate series of rules and regulations. This done, one could then enter a heaven, described in varying detail, some right down to who will sit where.

Studying these many descriptions of heaven, what heaven is like and who will reside there and who will be turned away at the gate, I couldn't help but notice the fiction creeping in. Since we cannot *know* what stamps will be required on our passports to eternity, we do the next best thing: we make them up. Humans are audacious beasts, bent on controlling and explaining the universe.

In the face of the unexplainable, the uncontrollable, we shift into fiction and create a story that gives us the power: Salvation For Dummies. Each of the stories I studied was exclusive; entrance to heaven would be attained only by following that story's tenets.

Then one day I read the words, "There are three thousand six hundred gates into heaven." I've forgotten the prophet (or pundit) who wrote it and the religion or philosophy that spawned it, but the words stay with me.

I like the idea. It feels right. I cannot conceive of any omnipotent being worth his salt who would be so narrow-minded as to haggle over the small print of contracts penned by mortals, many of whom, I suspect, have axes to grind. That would reduce the concept of salvation to game-show status: say the magic word and win eternal life. The magic word is Jesus, Muhammad, Buddha, Aphrodite—depending on where the contestant was born.

Once I decided that much of the conventional wisdom of established churches was driven by mortal turf wars and of no real consequence to God and me, I set out upon a long and continuing quest to make sense of good and evil, heaven and earth, spirituality and religion, life and death. (If nothing else, I have always dreamed BIG.)

As I have mentioned, it was a number or years of crashing and burning in the personal arena before I made the discovery that I was not God.

More years went by and I accepted that I cannot know the unknowable; that I must bring my beliefs into the kitchen, make them work in this world.

Finally I realized that though I was not God, I was *of* God. That's when the three thousand six hundred gates of my heart and soul began to creak open and the occasional breeze from heaven wafted into my life.

Where these metaphorical breezes originated, I have no idea. I do know the breezes touched me right here on earth. A foretaste of heaven? Or perhaps knowing I was of God, that each and every person place or thing around me was of God, is heaven. One of the many descriptions of heaven I've heard was given me by Sister Mary Judette: "An eternal moment in the love of God."

If the above is true and if one accepts (or suspects) there is a higher power, it follows that everything is of the one thing, either through creation or fragmentation. If this is so, then life on earth is part of this eternal moment, either a precursor to passing through one of the three thousand six hundred gates into heaven or a gate in and of itself.

I can't know what will happen when I get around to shuffling off this mortal coil. That must be left in the hands of God. Not knowing the unknowable, I cannot prepare for it. If you don't know what sport will be played, there's no sense packing a lot of equipment. What I can do is prepare my little corner of earth so that should He come to me in any form, He would be met with kindness and generosity, His creations taken care of to the best of my ability, His creatures, two- and four-legged, treated with respect. Attempting to echo, in my small human way, His grace is much harder than seeking a more esoteric heaven.

Since I cannot realistically seek Him in the afterlife or the cosmos, I will keep my eye out for Him in the neigborhood, try to be ever vigilant, assuming that everyone from the pizza delivery girl to the guy with the obnoxious all-terrain vehicle could be Him, or at least *of* Him. I will cultivate blessings and grace in the dirt of my garden, the words of my friends, the eyes of my dogs.

Then, when I die, should I fail to sneak through those pearly gates, I shall, at the very least, already have had a small taste of the love and joy said to abide there.

forgiveness

Forgiveness. What's that about? My sister and I have had numerous discussions on just what forgiving entails. Both of us are angry by nature, holding grudges in the coldest way possible by quietly shutting out of our lives those who have offended.

So how would forgiveness actually work? Would one remember the grievance but no longer care? If you no longer care, you no longer *care;* whatever it is ceases to be of importance. No forgiveness there: you just got over it.

Did one just forget it? Wipe it out of memory? A new slate? Forgetting evil done smacked of amnesia or some other mental illness. Surely forgiveness did not mean simply going into a pathological sense of denial.

Perhaps forgiveness was knowing that evil was done, still caring about it, but *pretending* not to mind. Another possibility was knowing, caring and, rather than feeling anger toward the doer, feeling pity. To our way of thinking both of these were based in hypocrisy and self-elevating condescension. Pretending injures the pretender and pity is a self-sanctified revenge on the perpetrator of the evil. Surely forgiveness, touted as such a fine and spiritual thing, was more than that.

As long as you remember, know, and feel evil's been done, it hurts. If you don't forget, ignore, outgrow, or lie about it, what's left?

Finally we came to the conclusion that there was no such thing as true forgiveness in any meaningful sense. The word was merely a polite way to cover hypocrisy, fear, and hatred; a sort of spiritual one-upmanship to make one seem better than somebody else and lessen the humiliation of being done to.

I was stuck with this logical, if cynical, conclusion for a long time, time in which I struggled with the weight of juggling the sharp-edged emotions that come with being hurt. Then one day, in church of all places, I had a revelation. The pastor was reading that bit in the Bible where Jesus says to His apostles: "That which you forgive, shall remain forgiven, that which you do not forgive will be retained." Or something along those lines.

From there I believe the sermon wandered off to discuss the apostles' new responsibilities. My mind took another direction. To me it sounded not as if a power to forgive or not to forgive was being bestowed but rather the apostles were being reminded, perhaps warned, that every transgression they did not forgive would be retained. Retained by them, by us, by me. Carried by me, fed, watered, and hauled from place to place by me.

Or I could forgive and be free.

The evildoer would continue to exist doing what he does, repenting or not.

I would continue to exist.

But the evil itself would be over, gone, done, history as in no longer is, not happening. I realized what had been alive and biting was not the original evil but my oft-rehearsed, dearly held memory of evil.

My definition of forgiveness is a sigh, very like a sigh of relief, on which the memory of evil is breathed out.

With letting go of the memory, discontinuing the incessant replaying of pain, and instead feeling the unmitigated *overness* of the evil, the evildoer often looks quite different: flawed, like me, a child of God, like me. Forgiven. Like me.

gratitude

Gratitude has gotten short shrift in American culture. Most of my favorite authors are long-dead English people. I love Dickens, Trollope, Austen, and all of the Brontë sisters. My friend Debra once defined optimism as "Walking into a bookstore thinking, 'Hey, maybe there'll be a new Jane Austen.'" I agree wholeheartedly.

One of the themes running through eighteenth- and nineteenth-century English novels is gratitude. Woven throughout the pages is the belief that kindness received from patrons is worthy of being repaid with lifelong loyalty and devotion.

This isn't the picture I get here at home. Oh, sure, we deal with gratitude fairly well on the small stuff. Please pass the salt. Thank you. What a nice tie. Thank you. But when it comes to the big gifts, an inner struggle ensues. In the unwritten code that dictates how Americans perceive their place in the social structure, it must be encoded that accepting a kindness—a handout—demeans the recipient. Charity is a dirty word; those who take it as well as those who give it are suspect. Giving and receiving are about power. The giver has it, the receiver hasn't. Power corrupts. Therefore, the giver's motives cannot be pure. Who does he think he is, playing lord of the manor? *What does he want in return?*

Shame comes with unearned gifts. To accept charity is to publicly admit you're a failure. If you do take charity, you've got to justify it in order to hold your head up. *It was owed me. Since he's so rich and I'm broke, he must've stolen it from me someway. He just wants to impress everybody at my expense. How dare he think this pittance is enough?*

According to my totally unscientific investigation, service has suffered the same fate. In America, there's no service tradition, no honor in being a servant, only in being a master.

In the fictional world of my old dead English friends, service and gratitude are respectable, honorable states and, though I coveted these mind-sets, I never could quite emulate them. The rule of capitalism, both social and fiscal, coupled with the American myth of rugged individualism, had locked me into a belief system where I rewarded myself only for strength, success. To be a good loser was, well, to be a *loser,* for chrissake.

It's probable I would have remained that way, surviving on arrogance, had my life not taken a serious turn for the worse, my marriage disintegrated; I was hurled into a black place. Never having been there before, I wasn't aware of when the normal insanity inherent in divorce changed, the scales tipped, and I dropped into full-blown clinical depression with its attendant grim festivities.

Paradoxically—or, perhaps, inevitably—it was from this dark place that I finally experienced the kind of gratitude I'd read about. Family and friends took care of me. They kept right on taking care of me through all the blood and wailing and tears. They listened to endless hailstorms of acid words, put things back together when I tore them apart, and never let their fears or frustrations turn them away from me.

Clearly they didn't do this because they wanted something from me. The state I was in, I was of no practical use to anybody. They certainly didn't do it to appear saintly. Sticking with me during those years was the act of madwomen. There was no power to be had; they were as powerless as I. No moral superiority existed to bask in. What fun is it to be morally superior to the mentally ill? It was done simply—or, more accurately, complexly and miraculously—out of love.

They just plain, flat-out loved me. Because of this, I lived and eventually got well.

As I grew stronger and the crippling self-absorption of depression began to wane, I discovered a new sensation had taken root: gratitude. True, joyous gratitude. A blossoming within that flowered into a deep and abiding desire to tend to the well-being of these most precious individuals. Not because I owe them. Because I love them with the kind of love they taught me. Experiencing the liberation of honest gratitude, I slowly began learning the inexplicable richness of servanthood. The unparalleled honor of serving others.

Today I live a life of gratitude and, though I fail at it as often as I succeed, I enjoy being of service, finding ways of expressing the exhilarating love that exists in and around me. I am fond of poring over the great goodnesses I was blessed to receive and the marvelous sensation of love for those who had the strength and courage to give them to me. The feeling of *owing* them has been transmuted into a feeling of loving them. Love begets love, it would seem, and the energy spent returning the grace they bestowed on me begins (oh so slowly for this imperfect woman) to ooze out onto those around me. First it was only to those I love, but then, to my surprise and delight, it began to spread to those I don't even know but share a kinship with because of remembered pain and knowledge of the joy I have in being helped to survive it.

I'm hard-pressed to say I'm glad I suffered clinical depression, but I am grateful even for the evils because of the incredible gifts that sprang from them.

sin

I simply adore sin and have sinned mightily in all categories: venial, mortal, sins of the flesh, sins of commission, sins of omission. As it says in the Book of Common Prayer, I have sinned against my neighbor and myself.

Because I love precision of ideas and words, I have given a good deal of thought to the subject, pondering the differences between the unethical, the immoral, and the sinful. Ethics, I can grasp; it's based on the concept of fairness learned in kindergarten. Though I have failed altogether too many times to behave ethically, I usually came to understand my wrongs and eventually tried in my own way to right them.

Sin and immorality hit differently. They brought out the rebel in me. Both smacked of control; rules developed by stiff-necked, hide-bound people, rules that had no basis but in the rulemakers' own repressed psyches and were designed to force their way of thought on others. Certain sins, the obvious biggies—thou shalt not kill, thou shalt not steal—the ones that had been transmuted into law to retain the security of the state and the individual, I accepted, but I accepted them as laws, not as sins. Judgment and penalty dealt out by the courts, not some mythical being or sanctimonious celibate.

"Sin" had the connotation of an evil above and beyond the act committed, an evil that somehow stained the soul, diminished the sinner in an elemental way, and could only be expunged through "grace."

This, I suspected was, yet again, a control measure taken by organized religions purporting to have detected a peculiar and debilitating disease for which only the mother church had the antidote. A handy way to keep the flock off balance and tithing. A petty set of rules, and I loathed rules.

I came of age in the sixties when the rules were gleefully overthrown. Old mores were being torn down. In desperation the adults repeated by rote what they'd learned. Some of it wasn't true, and that was reason enough for many of my generation to chuck out the bathwater, baby and all. Shaking free of the concept of sin seemed right and good and logical.

As a consequence, I stayed fairly legal and moderately ethical but chose to believe sin and immorality were mere constructs of outmoded social structures kept alive by those too scared to come bravely into the twentieth century.

Because I was so young, I had no real experience of consequences. The consequences of sin don't necessarily manifest in the short run, and I had intentionally deafened myself to anyone old enough to have seen sins come home to roost. Fornication, adultery, pride, sloth, coveting: these and a hundred others I deemed personal choices, statements of lifestyle.

In eschewing existing structures, I found myself without spiritual shelter or protection, with no way of avoiding the pitfalls.

And so I sinned and I sinned and I wondered why the hell my life wasn't working out all that well. After I wandered into that church and sat in the second pew under the window with the lilies and the lamb for several years, I surprised myself by saying to a congenital Christian, one born to it, "What I like about church are the *rules*."

Like many a good Christian, she replied, "What I *don't* like are the rules."

She'd never had to live without them. For thousands of years Jews and then Christians labored to hammer out a system for living together peaceably with others while keeping oneself spiritually whole and well. My generation had thrown this wisdom out and then tried to reinvent the wheel in a decade.

I looked again at sin with new eyes and an open mind.

I still don't believe sin is a God thing in the sense of recording and punishing. I doubt a Being that rules all-known galaxies and watches novas instead of late night TV is going to say: "Whoa, little Alice *French*-kissed that boy! Am I ever going to remember THAT!" No, God isn't going to lose much sleep if we covet our neighbor's wife. I do believe it's a God thing in the sense of wise counsel, guidance, a helping hand.

My feeling is, ninety-nine times out of a hundred, sins are simply really rotten ideas. Adultery is painful, expensive, and not nearly as much fun as you thought it would be. Coveting makes you bitter and angry, ill at ease with the neighbor and his wife. Living "in sin" keeps a lame-duck relationship that should have been over in six months limping along for two years. I could go down the list of all the seriously bad ideas we've been warned against but, if you're over fifteen, you've discovered they all have hidden costs.

I've reached the conclusion that sinning is much like drinking from a faucet with a Water Not Potable sign over it. You can do it. It's not illegal. God won't strike you down. But odds are you'll get sick.

addiction

When my sister and I were in our teens, we read a tabloid article that listed indicators by which one could identify aliens walking the earth in the guise of humans, and couldn't help but note that our mother exhibited eight out of ten of the telltale signs. We could never get her to admit to extraterrestrial ancestry but often wondered if it accounted for the fact that we never felt quite at one with our fellow human beings. As we walked and wandered in wider circles, it became evident that our very "otherness" was what we shared with the human race, this sense of "not quite"ness.

The more I observed, the clearer it seemed to me that human beings—and I now include myself in that group—are apparently born with, or soon develop, an emptiness, a vacuum, a dead zone at the core of their being.

For me, this emptiness was felt in the body as well as within the mind. It manifested as a hollow feeling—an ache without corporal pain—just behind my sternum, a drain through which contentment, satisfaction, and inner peace leaked away.

As far as I'm concerned, this dead zone is at the root of addiction. I've been a creature prone to addiction my entire life. As my friend Mari puts it: "I've had to give up more things than most people have ever tried." Love, chocolate, cats, cigarettes, alcohol, people, places, things, animals, vegetables, minerals: the only one that's never plagued me is addiction to work, and I suspect that has only been avoided because of my couch addiction. If something makes me feel better, dulls that spectral ache for a moment, lends a specious sense of belonging, then I wanted a whole lot of it and I wanted it often. Unfortunately, these various efforts to stop the leak were temporary at best and had side effects worse than the ephemeral pain.

I'd heard religious folk refer to this hollow feeling as a "God-sized hole" and use it to explain why every culture throughout history has needed to invent, discover, or appropriate gods. I suffered the hole and I admired the reasoning but remained unmoved. The religious types I noticed just used the image of a god like I used my various substances; merely another addiction with which to stop up the drain and one that worked no better and had just as many unpleasant side effects as booze or drugs.

However, close to thirty years of watching everything from caffeine to relationships disappear down this internal rat hole, I decided, what the hell, I'd tried everything else, why not give God a go? At least it was legal and nonfattening.

Once I entered into the fold, so to speak, I would occasionally run across someone who seemed to truly know God, and I realized that religion, like a bad toupee or a face-lift gone sour, is only obvious when it's done badly. For those doing it right, there seemed to be a continuity of peace and strength that was visible only in the kindness—tolerance, in the best sense of the word—shown toward others and toward themselves.

Bit by bit it dawned on me that this mental/spiritual/imaginary void within was not a hole that required stopping up but a sort of fuel tank, needing to be constantly refilled to power my life. Looking upon this hollowness as a hunger for sustaining power rather than a drain down which the good things went, I began to take note of the kinds of fuel I was in the habit of pouring in. Considering the garbage I dumped there, it made sense that my life force ran erratically, with jerks, racing, sudden stops, and a good deal of foul black smoke.

In realizing I fueled my spiritual self with garbage at best and poison at worst, I was afforded the barest glimmer of an inkling that better fuel was available.

With God, though He may be omnipresent, omniscient, and omnipotent, one size does not fit all. Each of us can only perceive Him with the senses we've been given, with our human hearts and minds and experiences. Surely, I thought, if He wanted to be heard and seen, He would make Himself known to each person in a form that individual could understand, be it a many-armed diva or a white male patriarch in flowing beard and nightgown.

I set out to find what sort of god would work with my idiosyncratic soul.

To this end I worked to open my self, clean away the junk, the obsessions, the metaphorical painkillers that shored up my ego, and let the hollow place stand empty. I practiced the Zen of breathing in and out. I tolerated the emptiness, resisted the urge to cram it full of whatever was handy. After some years, my heart was as often the residence of silence as of smoke and clamor. Acceptance, awareness, stillness, a sense of something greater than myself crept in. A comforting knowledge of belonging arose. Though I hadn't experienced it before, it was as familiar as the road leading home. By small increments, my life began to run more smoothly. I now enjoy not merely moments of peace but, when I'm lucky, entire days.

I would like to say that, upon understanding fully this concept of clean, environmentally friendly fuel for the soul, I attained permanent enlightenment, total serenity. But the old aching loneliness returns now and again and, with it, the knee-jerk desire to dull the sensation with some moderately toxic substance. Still, I am on the winning side. These times are fewer and farther between, the duration shorter, and the collateral damage remarkably small.

justification

Justification is an offshoot of the art of sophistry, obscuring the clean lines of truth with a complex overlay of words. Actually, I'm quite good at this. Because I am infernally lucky (or unbelievably blessed), I've been able to transmute this skill into a livelihood by writing fiction.

As a profession, it's worked well for me. As a woman striving to behave herself in an emotionally charged world, the practice of justification has stunted my growth, blinded me when I most needed to see, and allowed me to engage in more damaging behaviors than one conscience should be called upon to process in a single lifetime.

Justification requires words. One of the best ways to test if you are indeed justifying an inferior act is to stop talking. If the deed can stand alone in silence, it's probably okay. When the act is not right, we need words to tie the bad behavior to other more acceptable behaviors, as if the act we're justifying were a sinking ship being passed off as whole and functional by buoying it up with many floats. The ship can be kept above water, people can be fooled into thinking it's sound, but essentially it remains a wreck and, in a short while, becomes an anchor to the floats supporting it.

I've used all of the classic justifications: the ends justify the means, everybody else is doing it, you did it first, he had it coming, you gave me no other choice. My friend Mari, a creative soul, used to laugh at herself when she'd been backed into a corner. When the rest had been stripped away, her last-ditch justification was, "Okay, maybe I was wrong. But they didn't *handle* me right."

In *One Flew Over the Cuckoo's Nest,* Chief Bromden suffers when, in his psychosis, he believes a fog machine—the combine—has been turned on. This machine confuses, deceives, blinds, rendering the real and the unreal indistinguishable.

By accepting or indulging in justification, we turn on the fog machine. With a cloud of words and a web of spurious interconnections, what is real is obscured. The purpose is to deceive, to aggrandize ourselves, to obtain something unearned.

To deceive is to cheat. Cheating others is one wickedness;

cheating ourselves is another. By justifying bad acts we cheat ourselves of the lesson the act may have taught us. We cheat ourselves of the opportunity to make amends, enrich our lives, and strengthen our relationships. We cheat ourselves of the time and energy to do the right act, one that will work.

Justifications are labor-intensive. It requires a good deal of mental work and verbal skill to generate a plausible justification. And once the thing is created, the chore isn't over. Justifications are high maintenance. Keeping the illusion that that rotting hulk of an act is shipshape and ready to sail requires constant tending of floats and support lines.

Confession, on the other hand, though not sweet, is usually short: "I blew it. I was dead wrong. I'll do my best to fix it." When this is done, I may be forgiven or not, escape punishment or not, but the hit has been taken. A promise has been made to make amends to the best of my ability. Of course, if I do not fulfill my promise I am doomed to another exhausting round of buoying up a new wreck, justifying why I didn't make amends.

If I do manage to take the next step and actually fulfill this promise and do so genuinely and honestly the very best way I know how, I am done. I no longer have to work to support the insupportable, think to justify the unthinkable. The ball, however big or disgusting, is firmly in the other court.

And I am graced with the freedom to move on.

judgment

They say judgment awaits us all. You won't have to wait long if you are within a sixty-foot radius of me. Between the swimsuit aisle and the jewelry counter at Wal-Mart, I can make forty to fifty judgments: bad hair, lose the earring, ever heard of a *gym,* buddy?

I've always looked upon this as a harmless entertainment; after all, I never actually said any of those things. (Well, hardly ever . . .) Lately, though, I've begun noticing a strange side effect of my hobby. For a long time I've been aware of a mild frisson of superiority when judging others as less marvelous than I—probably why I kept on doing it—it's not like it pays the rent or anything. But in the last little while I've suffered a slightly bitter aftertaste, anger or resentment of some kind.

What brought this to my attention was my spurious judgment of a beloved friend whom we shall call "Bilbo." (I'm reading *Lord of the Rings* at the moment.) Bilbo, whom I love dearly, is in a relationship with a woman (whom we shall call "Frodo"), so lost in depression she is unable to think of anyone but herself. Recently Frodo threw another self-centered fit that spoiled a family event. Bilbo forgave her, justified her actions, and took a lion's share of the blame onto himself. In telling my husband this tale, I started judging Bilbo's actions and motivations. As I voiced my condemnations, I grew angry with my adored Bilbo, taking on what he and Frodo did, felt, and said as if it had something to do with me. In fanning this kernel of anger, a picture formed from the flames, a picture of Bilbo that was ugly. And that hurt.

For no reason except spitefulness and arrogance, I was tarnishing a solid gold friendship. My judgment was becoming my reality.

Since I never let a thought go unthunk, I thought about what I was getting out of pouncing upon and savoring aspects of others that could be seen as negative; why I wanted to see them in a negative rather than a positive—or better yet, neutral—light. Surely I wouldn't be crazed enough to engage in such an energy-intensive, emotionally expensive pastime if there wasn't a payoff. After serious contemplation it came to me that, in judging others, whether the judgment was positive or negative, I was one-upping the judgee. If the judgment was negative, that made me better than they were. If it was positive, then, as elevated as they might be, I was higher, in a position to pass judgment upon them. The attendant anger—in the long run the proverbial canker that gnaws—was in the short run a stimulant, like being scared at the movies. It gave a little burst of energy, made me feel more alive, added interest to my life. In my role as the Omniscient One, I could solve their problems while blissfully ignoring my own. I could condemn their weaknesses by pretending I didn't share them, that I would have done better, been smarter or stronger or saner. During the time I sat on the judge's bench, I was free of my own life and, in some petty way, in control of theirs if only in the sense of dictating what was wrong and what was right.

Escaping my own reality, ignoring my own sins, feeling better than others, and getting an energy boost are nice but, like other drugs, the fun doesn't last long and leaves a hangover with the half-life of plutonium.

We experience life not as it is but as we perceive it to be. When we perceive that banging sound out in the kitchen in the dead of night not as a cat trying to get into a cupboard but as that guy with a hook for a hand who escaped from an asylum near our old high school, we experience fear, genuine fear of the same caliber as if the cat really were the one-handed psycho. A casual glance from a passerby, when perceived as a rapacious leer, will trigger a feeling of shame or outrage. Because we have judged this glance to be unsavory, we respond just as if our virtue had really been assaulted.

We are responding not to what happened but to what we think happened. In reality, we don't know why the guy on the street looked at us in that way, Jenny made that remark, the pig in the SUV gave us the finger when changing lanes, Bilbo decided to stay in an abusive relationship, or Frodo must strike out at people. Most of the time we cannot know the whys of others' lives. We have a very limited knowledge of what *is;* all else is our own perception of what we *think* is.

By thinking bad things about others, by labeling their behaviors as crude, ugly, weak, or stupid, I was actually creating a whole lot of crude, ugly, weak, and stupid that I then had to live with. Before I passed judgment, the person was simply a person. By labeling them, I made the choice of what kind of person they would be in my world.

In *Hamlet* it is said: "There is nothing either good or bad, but thinking makes it so." I wouldn't go quite that far. There is plenty of wrong under heaven that I had nothing to do with. But it has proven true for me in many cases. Something merely is; I then judge it to be bad and suffer accordingly.

"So ye judge others, so shall ye be judged" and "judge not lest ye be judged" never had much impact on my behavior. The concepts were sufficiently vague and far enough in the future they couldn't deter any rottenness I was of a mind to commit in the now.

Feeling my love for Bilbo turning sour was immediate, personal, and painful. Goaded by the sting of my actions—all of which had taken place in the mind, then been given being by the words I'd spoken—I was forced into an acute awareness of the cost of judging others, the cost to Me. "So ye judge others, so shall ye be judged" ceased to be a biblical warning of confrontation at the pearly gates and became a simple statement of fact.

I judged Bilbo as being bad so, therefore, I felt bad. I had shined an ugly light on my friend and now my friend looked ugly to me. Cause and effect, one action bringing an equal and opposite reaction; not metaphysics but high-school physics.

I still judge people. It still amuses me and passes the time. But I've become wary of the entertainment, careful of the gossip I indulge in, because now I know when I next see this person I've been gleefully demeaning, I will see them not as they are but as I have painted them.

Then I will have to come to terms with the monster I have made.

turning the other cheek

Turning the other cheek was always an unattractive option to me. I was raised in ranching country. We all loved John Wayne—men, women, and kids. Though few of us could live it, the Code of the West permeated our lives: honor, courage, strength, no trespassing, and "smile when you say that, pardner."

A hit was an insult, a challenge and, if unanswered, an invitation to be walked over. The movies and the history I imagined for my rugged, hardworking father taught me that when hit, you hit back even harder.

Makes perfect sense to me. Anyone mean enough to strike me is probably not going to be gentlemanly enough to stop with one paltry cheek. Why make it easy for the SOBs? as my father would say.

Turning the other cheek struck me as very bad advice, indeed. Tossing the phrase on the garbage heap at the back of my mind, I continued to live gloriously at the movies with Dad and John. A Colt, not Jesus, would be my savior.

Year by year, the lesser hits—the real day-to-day kind lacking in drama and high stakes—began to reveal flaws in my pugnacious philosophy. Fighting fire with fire was only efficacious in certain wilderness conditions and then only if the wind and weather were right. An eye for an eye, a tooth for a tooth, soon rendered both parties blind and wearing dentures.

Hostile words, met with hostile words, bred only a continuance and escalation of hostilities. I never walked away from a verbal confrontation feeling good. Sometimes I'd feel justified, smug, maybe even victorious, but there was that creepy, hollow adrenaline burn of anger that could last for days, sometimes weeks, where I'd have to rehash the incident again and again, bettering my part in it. The incident was never over when it was over; I carried it with me.

Slights, petty remarks, road-rage incidents, snitty sales clerks, the slings and arrows that soured my everyday life—pinpricks too mundane for Hollywood, too petty for John Wayne—had a habit of spreading from the point of origin like ugly stains.

A rude driver cutting me off in traffic made me bitter. Striking back, I'd snap at a slow salesgirl and watch her turn sullen and angry, ready to pass the ugliness on to her husband, her child, the next customer. As I watched this process unfold again and again, pieces of a new/old concept began to appear on the edges of my mind.

The pieces were finally knocked into place by a big hammer. I was watching an interview with a Serbian woman on CNN. The newsman spoke to her over the fresh corpse of her son, killed in the seemingly endless war. I couldn't help but feel sorrow for one so bereft of one she loved. The Serbian woman grieved and wailed, then said: "My husband was killed in this war, and my son. Now I will raise his son to fight and die." At that a great deal of my compassion evaporated.

I thought, "Holy smoke, woman, no wonder you spend all your leisure time at funerals."

And it came to me: turning the other cheek, taking the hit, absorbing it, not striking back with your body or your spirit, effectively says, "The violence stops here, with me. I take it. I hold it. This stream of hate will flow no farther."

Taking in this pain and containing it were not acts of cowardice or victimhood but of great courage, tremendous strength. Once I'd done this successfully I found true honor lay in stopping the cycle, being the one to take the hit not only for myself but for those who would be infected should I pass it on.

I'm sure, with an enlightened scriptwriter, this is what John Wayne would have done.

prayer

In the play *Sister Mary Ignatius Explains It All for You,* Sister Mary talks about prayer. She says (paraphrased), "You think your prayers aren't answered? They are. It's just that sometimes the answer is NO."

This struck me as terribly amusing and telling because, for all intents and purposes, there's no proof prayers are answered. Sure, sometimes I prayed for things and they happened. Mostly I prayed and they didn't happen: the cat didn't come back, my sister-in-law didn't forgive me, it rained on the day of my big event. I know for a fact God wouldn't get me an acting job when I needed one and, if He did have a hand in getting my first book published, He sure as hell took His own sweet time about it.

A Lutheran minister I know once said prayers come in two categories: help me, help me, help me, and thank-you, thank-you, thank-you. I was stuck in help me for a long time. I prayed for relief in the form of things, people, jobs. Some of those prayers were "answered," some were not. Of those things I begged for that did come to pass, some were good for my life, and some turned out to be a real bad idea.

So, what's the point? This god of prayer was more or less an imaginary punching bag when I was unhappy and a vague target at which to hurl my thank-you notes when I was on a roll.

And what's this about "God will never give you a cross too heavy for you to bear"? What a crock. We're given crosses too heavy to bear all the time. We become alcoholics, kill ourselves, kill other people, go insane. Even Christ, nailed on the quintessential cross, cried out, "My God, my God. Why hast thou forsaken me?" He just couldn't hack it a minute longer.

"God knows what's best for us" is another axiom that, though soothing for some, doesn't work for me. Is war best? Murder, rape, torture, are they best? Nope. I couldn't help but prefer Sister Mary Ignatius's god who simply said "no" and made no excuses.

As long as I thought of God as a cross between Superman and Santa Claus with a cell phone and myself as a lobbyist for my own needs, I was doomed to atheism, confusion, and resentment.

The concept of a personal meddling god, one who listens to our prayers and, like Dear Abby, either answers personally or has one of his minions attend to it, though comforting, led only to frustration. When I clung to this image of god, I invariably became angry and rebelled against this capricious and often cruel "father." It made prayer a crapshoot with unpublished odds. One definition of insanity is doing the same thing over and over yet expecting different results each time. Given this, the above-discussed practice of prayer is the pastime of the lunatic gambler.

Yet I do pray. I still use help me, help me, help me and thank-you, thank-you, thank-you. What has changed are my expectations and my requests. At least those are the intellectual aspects. The sea change has been in my internal vision of God and how He interacts with me and my world; my *sensation* of the divine, how God lives in my body, and that twilight zone between mind and soul. At first I'd thought abandoning the concept of a God who would get me jobs, cure my ailing cats, and watch over me as I slept would leave me in a lonely place; that the *laissez-faire* god whose existence would be so impersonal as to be of no use to one small, middle-aged woman.

However, as I let go of the idea that God runs the corporeal world and not only sees every sparrow that falls but personally knocks the poor little sucker off his perch, I was able to grow calmer, cease my whining petitions. I started to listen. Accepting that the material world runs itself and God is of the spirit—a spirit that dwells in and acts through living things—the question of why God lets bad things happen to good people even when we expressly ask Him not to became moot.

Things of the world are by, for, and *of the world.* Those of us in the world, coupled with the laws of physics and meteorology, make things happen. We build and destroy. We grant wishes and smash dreams. God may watch, may even be interested for all we know, but the corporeal stuff of life—money, cancer, food, shelter, skiing—doesn't seem to be His bailiwick. Near as I can tell, He pretty much leaves this stuff to us.

His is the realm of the spirit.

Now I pray for things *of* the spirit: compassion, strength, guidance. I pray for the spirit to sustain me when the world sucks and to grace me with humility and generosity when I hit a winning streak. Nowadays, more often than not, my prayers are answered. And the answer is yes.

fear

Fear is my least-favorite emotion, worse even than despair. At least, when in despair, I can watch old black-and-white movies and eat chocolate. Fear renders me unable to taste, swallow, focus, or sleep. Fear jangles through the cells of my body like a cold electrical current short-circuiting the natural flow of life.

When I was twenty, I dropped acid. For me there was no Lucy in the Sky with Diamonds, no pretty colors or deeper understanding of a rose. It was, in the parlance of the day, a bad trip. Fear, like an all-encompassing, all-pervasive, malevolent creature, entered my mind and body. For four or eight or sixteen hours my soul was, in essence, a single, prolonged, frozen scream.

The drug finally wore off but, when I returned to myself, I was no longer safe anywhere. The fear had taken root. My brain had been carved, new ruts worn into the gray matter, where fear would pour down in sudden flashfloods. In the drop of a tab I had condemned myself to thirteen years of crippling anxiety attacks.

Because I must know or, if I can't know, at least seek, why things happen, I began an ongoing study of fear in hope of finding a cure for my affliction. During those years I sought neither medication nor therapy, because my terrors, having been triggered by the taking of a drug that rendered me insane, centered around two things: taking drugs of any kind and being found out for the lunatic I'd become. Should I share my anxiety attacks with anyone, I believed I would be labeled crazy and locked away in a nut house.

Eventually, a therapist I'd gone to see for unrelated reasons discovered my secret and, with work, the attacks went away.

My fascination with fear remained. Just what in the hell are we so afraid of? Is fear mostly a physiological thing: heart rate goes up, skin crawls, sphincters slam shut or fly open? Is it adrenaline or some other chemical poured into the system that triggers the sensation? Or is the world a genuinely terrifying place?

Since my fear was born from a single drop of windowpane LSD served up on a perforated square of paper, when it came it poured in like acid, battery acid, but with a cold fire that burned deep. A thought, a picture in my mind, the words of a stranger telling a frightening tale would come into me and I would be afraid. That something which buffers the heart from the demons was gone and each and every pointy-horned, scaly-tailed imp had access to my inner sanctums.

Acid drips from the surfaces of our world in a constant stream: media tales of horror, books recounting endless torturous deeds, magazines predicting evils from flabby thighs to coronary heart failure carried on a single French fry. Fear of heights, flying, death, public speaking, bad breath, poverty, abandonment, sickness, humiliation, boredom: the list is as long as the human experience.

With nothing to stand between us and this corrosive rain, we live our lives on the run or in hiding. We try to build up walls to keep us safe. Walls of booze, drugs, work, justification, anger. We try to control everything around us: lock the doors, pass laws, buy cell phones, move to gated communities, avoid unfamiliar people and places, make money. But we're never safe. Fear that the walls will be breached haunts us, drives us to dig that extra moat within the ramparts.

I did not want to live in my own captivity, a prisoner behind battlements I had built, kept inside by the remembered sound of demons at the gates.

There was a time, before the acid, when fear was a good thing, a sharp poke in the ribs that kept me from leaping off high walls, diving into waters too deep for me. A time when there were no petty demons, only pain earned and lessons learned, a childish time when I lived in the moment, not worrying over yesterday or fretting over tomorrow.

A time when I had faith.

Faith. This is where things get murky. Fear I can describe in intimate detail: how it feels, where it comes from. Faith is too complex. It's easy to drift off into prettily phrased vagaries that, in essence, mean nothing. Faith is unquestioning belief, complete trust, reliance. What kind of a thinking person with any experience of the world can have faith in anything but that the demons are out there and one must be very afraid? The faith I had before the acid burned it away was not in God or gods. Though I had faith in my parents, I was old enough to know I must stand on my own. My faith was simple, at least simple in retrospect. I had faith that I was a good, solid, functioning bit of the universe. Faith that I was pretty good at the job of being me. Faith that that was enough. Anything more was just icing on the cake.

That's the faith I headed back to. When I could be comfortable that I fit into the little hole in the puzzle that was mine to fill, I found I stopped having to watch over myself with such vigilance. Every now and then I began to be able to look around, see other people, enjoy the sights, maybe even be of service.

So how did I make this miraculous leap from fear to faith? It wasn't a leap; it was a trudge, a tramp, a forced march. Years of painful deconstructing of the walls, letting the demons and imps come in, feeling the bite and claw of their wretched little claws, being stomped by their nasty little hooves, and then noting with wonder and joy that not only had I lived through my terrors, I was still relatively sane.

From fear to faith was a journey of letting go for me. Letting go not of the fears but of the defenses I'd constructed against them. Succumbing to the terror, letting it wash over me in waves, then getting up again to marvel I was in one piece. After many near drownings, the fear began to lose its power, I knew its parameters and knew I could handle them.

As the fear diminished, the belief that I was competently filling that tiny Nevada-sized hole in the universe began to trickle back. Belief let me walk through the world with a sense of belonging, of completeness, that I was, if nothing else, adequate at being me. And that that is a good enough beginning.

stillness

Life jangles. Noise is constant: traffic, dishwashers, TVs, airplanes, music, voices and voices and voices. Words clatter in my ears and brain. When the voices outside are quiet, voices in my head prattle. Conversations I've had, might have, should have had rattle on like a nonsense play in which I act all the roles, constructing or revising realities that never existed, never will.

We've grown so accustomed to this cacophony that a lot of us feel empty and not a little uncomfortable when the clamor stops. To be alone, in sudden silence, feels like abandonment, not peace but dead calm. It's as if the noise in our lives, the constant interaction with others, though it takes place only in our heads, keeps us connected, keeps us from drifting without an anchor in a lonely sea. And it most certainly keeps us from having to be alone with ourselves.

To cut wood and haul water, as Zen teaches—the simple act of living, committing to the job at hand, dwelling within the moment that is real and true—becomes not only difficult but somehow frightening and we run to rejoin the buzz of the hive. Cell phones are the ultimate symptom of this aberration. We seem so in need of constant contact, constant stimulation, that we cannot even drive to the market without plugging into the Borg nerve center. The Borg, you Trekkies will know, is/are a people little better than automatons, made half of machinery, half of flesh, who exist as a single entity, their minds and souls in constant contact with the mother ship. A people who do not think or even feel for themselves. In essence, there is no "self." There is only the Borg, a soulless web of eyes and ears and hands.

The rush and yak gives a sense of importance; the exhausting yet aggrandizing illusion that life will not go on, work will not be completed, children will fail, and friends go astray without our constant fuss and management. It has become fashionable to be too busy, a bragging point to be harried and overworked. Multitasking is touted as desirable, "having it all" considered attainable. Not to be constantly doing, always talking, marks one as less successful than her rushing, nattering peers. Maybe without the yammer of our imaginary importance we're afraid there would be no self, just . . . nothing, so we're desperate to keep up the constant rain of words, trudging through a fog of aimless chatter and mind-numbing worries, eating without tasting, hearing without listening, looking without seeing.

In noise and interaction there may be connection in the most rudimentary sense of the word, but there is no *relationship.* To truly relate—to self, to others, to the God of our understanding—there must first be stillness.

The truth is we cannot know God but through those gifts we have been given: eyes, ears, mind, heart. To have any sense of our relationship with God we must first relate to who we are, where we are, when we are. This precise moment in time and life is all we can know of anything. This moment is where God and self meet.

Without entering consciously into stillness, I cannot feel anything greater than myself. Even prayer is often just a continuation of the endless monologue in my skull, a rehearsing of my needs, hopes, expectations; not so much a relationship with the divine as "Dear Diary, send help."

Be still and know that I am God.

For those of us cursed with a monkey-mind, the first part of the command is hard to achieve. To be still; still in body, still in mind. Much of my life has been spent in a waking dream, my mind full of yesterdays and tomorrows while I slept through today.

To build a relationship I must learn to experience what *is.* I must be here, now. I must stay awake, genuinely see people, hear their words. How can I possibly be with anyone in any meaningful sense if I cannot even be aware of my own real life?

It takes two to enter into a relationship. In not knowing myself, in not being centered and in touch with myself, my own feelings, needs, and wants, there's no way for me to relate. There is no central integral "me" to begin the process. Others are left not relating to a whole person but to a scattered collection of aphorisms, worries, and words that don't add up to much.

Even over the distance of time and space that separates you and me, I can hear the "buts" beginning to percolate up like the empty bubbles in a coffee pot: but, but, but I *have* to, but they *expect* me to, but if I *don't*. . . . In essence, when I say those things, I am saying: "I am too important to stop. I am too important to take the time for this 'knowing God' nonsense." I am giving into the belief that all I have to offer is the running of errands, commenting on the lives around me. I am not offering myself, merely my time and my attention.

In living that way I condemn myself to a life of hurried littles.

My grandmother, may she rest in peace, when she thought I was getting too big for my britches, would often say: "Put your finger in a bucket of water, pull it out, and see just how big a hole it leaves." Once I was able to accept that I was not the generating power behind my life, understand and actually come to embrace my relative unimportance in the universe, I experienced an exhilarating freedom; freedom to stop the clamor, step back, and live this moment of life. With my mind clear and my eyes open, I can relate to others and not merely to the roles I assigned them in my mental theatrics. And I can relate to myself and not merely respond to the roles I sense others projecting onto me. I see that not only am I real but others are just as real as I am. Compassion comes more easily. Understanding replaces anger. Patience is not so hard-won. I am *relating,* and it's heaven.

This exercise in staying awake for my own life is ongoing. A hundred times a day I have to turn down the volume of the static in my mind, take a breath, separate myself from the racing rats, and return to my own skin. The stillness that exists in these moments serves as a constant warp that clarifies and makes cohesive the bright busy weft of everyday life. Without it, there is no form, no pattern to my existence, merely a long run on a treadmill going nowhere.

humility

There are two concepts regarding humility that I pretty much adhered to in my younger days. On an early *Star Trek* episode, when Kirk was still captain, Q, a superbeing, said something to this effect: "It's hard to work and play well with others when you're omnipotent." The other was from Mordred in *Camelot:* "The meek don't inherit the earth, they inherit the dirt." I was young and strong and smart and I couldn't see the point in pretending I was inferior to anybody. I distinctly remember another quote that I chose to ignore. I overheard a friend's mother saying, "Nevada is a nice girl, but she doesn't know her place." In my arrogance, I assumed she thought as I did and the statement was made to indicate that my place, wherever it was, was most certainly beneath hers.

Humility is all about knowing your place, being the right size for whatever role you've been handed at any given moment in life. When I am on tour, speaking to the public, it is my place to control the event. People come from their homes to hear me, and it would be a disservice to them should I let a member of the audience take over the event with their stories. When I'm standing in the parish hall eating finger sandwiches, I must remember that the Nevada Barr Show is over, that other peoples' need to tell their stories is of the same size as mine and must be treated with respect.

In our culture it is hard to know what the right size is. I was raised to think I loomed quite large on life's horizon, that, in essence, I was bigger than nearly everybody else: smarter, quicker, cleverer. Others I've met suffered a different fate and were taught to believe they were the smallest of God's creatures and their tiny squeaking voices should never be heard.

Humility comes from the root word *humus,* or earth. The dictionary goes on to define it in all the ways I'd known it: of low estate, self-abasing, absence of pride. I choose to return to the root, to the earth. A sense of knowing where my roots are, where my power stems from and, most important, of knowing that others are planted in the same soil, that regardless of how tall I've grown or how far my branches have spread, I am nurtured and sustained by the same good earth as my neighbors.

As a young actor, associating almost exclusively with other young actors, I experienced and witnessed the disappointment that a lack of humility sets us up for. It was *de rigueur* to believe we were God's gift to the world. I remember, when I got my first glimpse of humility, and said to a group: "I've come to realize I am not special, at least not more special than anyone else." They looked at me with a mix of pity and scorn. Finally one woman voiced her concern: "Well *I* am," she said. Even then I could hear an underlying desperation and anger in her words. By stating that I was not special, I had broken the code. If I was not, perhaps I thought she was not. Unacceptable.

At the time I didn't have the words to explain the relief at dropping the pretense (a pretense sustained not so much for others as for myself) that I was so much larger than I was; a hissing kitten with its fur fluffed out, a bullfrog with its throat blown up to frighten away the predators. It was amazingly comfortable to let the inner posturing go and just be my own size. I was also at a loss to explain how this revelation of my own size did not mean I thought any less of myself, took less pride in my achievements, or abandoned dreams of greatness. The contrary was true. The effort of sustaining and defending my inflated self-image left me constantly weary and anxious. When others didn't see the greatness of Me, niggling doubts that I was really a paper tiger gnawed at me. Anger at a world that refused to see me as *big* suffused relationships and often caused me to be belligerent, bitter. Most exhausting of all, keeping up the façade gave me an almost constant burden of self-consciousness. Everything I did or said had to be examined, weighed, and judgment passed upon it to see if it fit in with the image I wanted to project. What others said to me, how they looked at me went through a similar process. Did they see me as I wanted them to? With all these mental gyrations going on, I sounded stiff and awkward even to my own ears. Public gatherings, particularly if there was a director or producer there whom I wanted to impress, became an agony. I was lost, scrabbling to force myself into spaces where I didn't fit.

I didn't know my place.

Not knowing, I had the feeling of being a fly buzzing and banging into a windowpane, frustrated, alone, kept outside. On the occasions I was in, I had nothing but scorn for the other insects battering against the glass.

When I stumbled upon the sensation of true humility, of coming back to the earth, many of the unpleasant machinations vanished with no effort on my part. Simply because I made myself aware of my true size, of my rootedness in the common soil, much of the discomfort of relating to others melted away. It was sort of the feeling I'd get when a morning fog would burn off and the sun would come out. I could see more clearly, the chill damp on my skin evaporated. I was in my place and that place was unassailable, because it was intrinsically, idiosyncratically mine. My roots were there.

Now and again I am assaulted by great balloons of self-importance. I can feel them tugging, trying to pull me out of my native soil, separating me from the earth till I hang unbalanced, without anchor. With practice, I am getting better at recognizing the phenomenon, letting loose my inflated visions of Me. When I can do this, my sense of belonging, of safety, returns.

spiders and old men

A confluence of events caused a minor rebellion in me the other day. I was raised *right:* respect your elders, don't interrupt, be a good listener—all the stuff in which young girls are instructed. Until recently, I was pretty obedient in these areas. Then I killed a spider and an old man held forth till my little high-heeled footsies were aching fit to die.

Unlike the spider, the old man survived his meeting with me. We'd gone to an event held in honor of a friend of mine where this man—a local hero—was speaking. This fellow, a delightful and talented man, delivered an unplanned and undisciplined "speech," rambling on for an unconscionable length of time while the captive audience, only a blessed few of whom had the luxury of chairs, stood on one foot, then the other, wondering whether it would be the heat or the boredom that caused them to topple over first.

A little girl, five years old and so not yet in servitude to manners and formality, wriggled and crawled about, finally ending up on the floor with her stuffed bunny. She was the living manifestation of the audience's id. We all wanted to wriggle and squirm, play with our own toys and be comfortable. But the man would not shut up. By the time he wound down and his voice trailed off, I was positively crabby. Excessively crabby. Hostile even.

Since this servitude to the tedious blabbing of others was in no way a new experience—I have been cornered at cocktail parties, held hostage in doorways and on street corners while someone with no concern for anything but the sound of their own voice talked till my eyes rolled back in my head and my tongue began to protrude—I was not quite sure why this time I had such a violent reaction.

Then I killed this little spider. The spiders and I have an agreement—at least I have agreed to it; they seem to ignore the pact—outside, spiders live. Inside, they die with merciful quickness at my hand. This particular spider was scuttling about in an area of the treaty that hadn't been mapped out. She was in the car. Not really *inside* but not truly *outside* either. Not wishing to feel or imagine eight tiny hairy feet crawling on my person, I dispatched her with a napkin from Burger King.

Oddly, I felt rather bad about it. I could have put her out the window. Or even left her alone. Outweighing her by a good one hundred twenty pounds, had she tried to attack, I probably would have come out the winner. But, then, she was just a bug, for all her legs and eyes. And not the first spider to rue a run-in with me.

For some reason, this time, my mind turned on the fact that I had snuffed out a life. A skittery, biting, shriek-making life, to be sure, but still. . . . The spider had had that indefinable spark that made it alive, and I had quenched it. I wasn't in a morass of guilt and repentance, mind you. This was, after all, a spider who had technically, if not in spirit, broken the agreement, but the wonder of that life, however unpleasant to me, kept tickling around in my thoughts. Life is one thing we cannot create or replace. We don't understand it, not really. The difference between the quick and the dead remains one of the great mysteries.

Another thing we cannot create or replace is time. (Those of you who believe in eternal life might want to skip the rest of this and move on to another piece. For those of us less sanguine about what comes next, time is, as they say, of the essence.) Each of us has an allotted time of life. As I get older, that allotment gets shorter and shorter and, so, more precious. Time and life begin to merge, to be one and the same thing. Who bothers to bury the dead with their wristwatches on? In many senses, time *is* life. Time is the passing through, the celebration of, the curse of being alive.

The blabbering man had robbed me of this most valuable and irreplaceable of things: because of his insensitivity and self-centeredness, he'd gobbled up a great chunk of my time. There was no sharing of time or enhancing of life; he merely poured hard-to-hear, boring words out till I slipped into a standing coma wishing only that the time would pass. My time. My life. Wishing it away.

At the very bad part of my life which I have alluded to here and there, I ended up in a clinic for depression. This place was big on abuse and many there were walking wounded, people who'd suffered emotional, physical, sexual, verbal and other abuses. It was mentioned at one session that to talk *at* or be talked *at* without cease, without consideration, without allowing the participation of the other was a form of abuse.

At the confluence of the old man and the murder of my spider this came back to me with a clunk. Ah, yes! Abuse! Now I had the righteousness of the victim to rely upon.

The good child part of me, the sort of neo-Christian ethic that's been creeping up, argues for self-sacrifice, for abnegating personal desires to the needs of others. In church last Sunday we were told Jewish law said one must forgive three times. Christ is purported to have suggested seventy times seven. In other words, a whole, whole lot.

I am with the Jews and the psychologists on this issue. Any more than three times for those who bulldoze with words is not forgiveness but enabling.

I've decided not to let time-eaters consume bits of my life. Of course, one cannot take this to extremes, we are social creatures and some of this is unavoidable both in the giving and the receiving, but I have begun to practice gracious Southern ways of escaping. ("Why bless your heart, that's all very interesting, but I promised my Sunday school class I'd pray for 'em at seven-thirteen tonight.")

Mostly I try and be aware of the value of the time and life of those around me, to avoid being late, cancel call waiting, stop talking when I've nothing to say; to respect the sanctity of time and of life, mine and everybody else's.

marriage

Marriage is a subject I flunked the first time I took it. Since then I've had a great deal of time to think about what it means and what I did wrong and what is in my power to do right now that I am married for the second (and, one hopes, the last) time.

From day one, or as close to day one as my faulty memory can come, I'd been told that marriage was about commitment. This information came usually from the married: parents, grandmothers, teachers. The movies and books said it was about love. The poets said love conquered all. Happily Ever After was the prognostication of the fairy tales. Seldom did anyone explore what happened after that walk down the aisle. No one suggested that had Romeo and Juliet not died, they might have been divorced by the time they were thirty. Marriage was the blackout at the end of the scene, the implication being that some vague happiness, like death but better, was to unfold. Girls of my generation dreamed of the wedding, the racier ones dreamed of the wedding night. Nobody gave much thought to the morning after.

Having now lived through, all totaled, over seven thousand mornings-after, I have discovered that the parents were right: it's about commitment. In the sixties and early seventies when I was coming of age, commitment was a dirty word, right up there with "Republican" and "Establishment." It carried with it a negative connotation of giving up things, hopes, dreams. One was "committed" to insane asylums. Marriage was seen as the end of self-actualization because it denied one the freedom to know (in the biblical sense, naturally) other people.

In my first marriage, I sincerely believed I was committed. I believed that I would attain this mysterious "self-actualization" (then perceived more as self-aggrandizement than anything deeper) with my husband; that we would rise like two bright stars, the envy of all who beheld us. For about seven years this worked like a dream. Then our intensely parallel interests began to diverge and things fell apart. There was no room in my picture of marriage for the natural growth and separation that maturity demands. My vision of marriage shattered and, with it, my commitment. I had been committed not to him or myself but to a fantasy of *us.* When he abandoned that fantasy in his growth,

I felt lost and abandoned. Had I been genuinely committed to my husband, I would have found ways to facilitate that growth within the boundaries of marriage. Instead, I set out to find a new *us* in which to continue the fantasy of eternal bliss and oneness.

This, predictably, ended in total disaster.

In the years since, I have rethought commitment. My head was full of negatives: making do, settling, giving up, making the best of it. The concepts, to me, meant choosing to be less than. With the passing of time and thought, I've come to believe that commitment is about choice. Putting all your eggs in one basket, then *watching that basket.* Everything in life is a choice. If you want to be a concert pianist and a world-class boxer, early on you must choose one and abandon the other. To try and do both will end in the failure of both. To achieve one's best requires focus and dedication: choosing one thing, understanding the demands and parameters of that thing, and working within them to attain the desired goal. Marriage is such a choice. Not merely choosing the mate but choosing the life where personal growth and achievement are to be done within the parameters of an exclusive relationship; in which the health and happiness of both partners is of equal importance to the well-being of the union. Within these parameters, one partner cannot achieve personal satisfaction without the sustained health of the other and, so, of the marriage.

Oddly enough, in choosing this box, this institution, instead of feeling constrained and limited, I experienced real freedom. When a choice is made to focus on one thing, the necessity of keeping a myriad of other balls in the air diminishes. No longer am I required to meet, greet, date, wait by the phone, flirt, wonder, fantasize, worry—all the slings and arrows attendant in the mating game. I am home. Once I dedicated myself to making this home a beautiful and zestful place, my life was transformed. Tending to my husband's needs and wants has become inseparable from tending to my own. Both are necessary to keep my home rich and alive and joyful. In my own growth, I find that limiting myself to the "confines" of marriage in reality translates into the freedom to focus clearly on what I want, the fog of indecision in so many other matters is cleared away, allowing me to see each new direction I wish to take in building an exciting life and lasting relationship. The energy once spent on pursuing a fantastical happiness through my "perfect" mate or finding the proper stranger can now be used to garner real joy in the warmth of my home.

America is about freedom of choice. What I didn't understand till late in the game was that there is great freedom *in* choice. That boundaries are not limits but aids in focus, guardrails in unsafe environments, a warm place to run to when the world threatens to overwhelm me.

If this sounds too good to be true, it is. Only on paper can a marriage be perfect. Any organism, allowed to grow and change, must suffer through awkward stages, uneven spurts, plateaus, bad times. But if committed to weathering these without breaking the matrimonial bonds, I feel I'm working always with a safety net and the fear of falling is no longer crippling.

lies

There's something addictive about lying. I'm not talking about the Big Lies. Mostly we know we're in hot water when we find ourselves lying big. Either we're ashamed of what we've done because we know it was rotten, or we don't think it was rotten but lie because we haven't the moral rectitude to face the consequences of our choice. And I'm not interested in discussing Little White Lies. If you're old enough to read this book, you're old enough to know the difference between lying because you're a coward or a sneak and lying because your cousin doesn't need to know her thighs look like packing crates in spandex.

It is hoped one eschews the Big Lies and understands the need for White Lies. Their very obviousness forces us to be aware of them even if we've not the fortitude to eschew the former or the generosity to commit the latter.

It's the quiet lies that seduce. The little ones, cute, baby lies that "hurt" no one: shaving a second or two off your time running the mile, a few dollars off that dress you bought on sale, five pounds off your weight on your driver's license, making that nasty comment someone made just a wee bit nastier in the telling. A friend of mine, in the early stages of true addiction, referred to this habit as "tuning up the truth."

I wish I could say I have risen above this petty pastime, and always tell the truth, the whole truth, and nothing but the truth but, alas, this is not the case. At times, though aware of the slippery slope I tread, I still find myself altering the facts just a hair to make myself seem a bit taller, stronger, or more clever. The strange thing about this litany of "adjustments" is that they do not achieve the desired goal; they are too small, too insignificant to truly aggrandize.

Though not totally honest, since I discovered, some twenty-odd years ago, that I had developed the habit of lying, I have managed to curb it with some success. In and of themselves my tiny lies were relatively harmless to the listeners, but they worked against me in a myriad of ways; my credibility was subtly undermined over time and, once accustomed to lying in little ways, when time came and a Big Lie tempted, it was so much easier to tell it.

The greatest danger, though, was the boiling of the frog.

It's said (and I assume it's true) that if you put a frog in a pan of water and heat it slowly, the frog will not notice the changing temperature; he'll never hop out and save himself but will sit there till he boils to death. In telling the little lies, I slowly inured myself to the concept of honesty. It was so easy to start exaggerating the exaggerations, moving into the realm of lies that can be detected (thus looking like a liar and a fool), then into lies that could harm. The truth became malleable, unimportant, and, finally, meaningless.

Without a strong attachment to the truth, I was without anchor. What is, what happened, how it happened is what anchors me to life. I'd once thought that genuinely living in the moment, totally just in the one moment currently happening, would be the ideal. Then I saw a medical show which profiled a man with a head injury, an injury which manifested in the man's total inability to recall the recent past. This poor man would ask a hundred times in a twenty-minute conversation: "And who are you? Where am I?" Requests, asked and granted, were forgotten and asked again. He was totally in the moment, but without his past the moment had no depth, no weight, no meaning.

Lying let me detach myself from my past, my *real* past, and that is who I am. I am the woman who weighs one hundred twenty-one pounds, not the fictitious one-hundred-eighteen-pound woman on my driver's license. In a sense, the truth is as a million threads of varying thickness that tether us to who we are and where we belong in the world. There are times when I've wanted to escape my own reality, when the little lies (and the big ones) felt necessary. I needed to create another person because the one I'd found when I looked in the metaphorical mirror was not a woman I admired. But the lies couldn't change the image. They simply blurred it for me and made it too clear to those to whom I lied.

I've come to rely on the old saw that honesty is the best policy. Honesty in all things, great and small. Leaving no truth unturned. In my endeavor to be brutally honest, I expected to be hit constantly with the consequences the little lies were meant to ameliorate. The reverse has proved true. In telling the truth, I began to accept myself as is, warts and all. In accepting myself, I started to become free to *be* myself. The freedom I'd experienced when I was younger to enjoy my own idiosyncrasies, face my own limitations, take on projects I was admittedly ill-equipped to handle, and learn from others seeped back into my life.

To my great surprise, telling the truth, always and in painstaking detail, made me comfortable in my own skin, attuned to my own needs and wants, firmly tethered to my past, and hopeful about a future that would bring genuine strength and insight.

Others became more accepting of me as well not only because I disappointed them less frequently but because I let them see who I was, come to genuinely know me, even the bad things, the weaknesses. In admitting my faults, friends became able if not to help me, then to understand and so forgive more easily.

Whoever said, "And the truth shall set you free" knew what he was talking about.

religion

From my unscientific study of mankind it has become obvious to me that we are creatures who need ritual. Dervishes whirl, Pentecostals speak in tongues, Masai warriors leap. A chant, a dance—something seems to be required to assist us into a state where we can drop the everyday concerns and let our minds loose to explore the spiritual realm.

Being human, alive for only a brief moment and, so, impatient, we've sought a shortcut to all this and come up with drugs. People have dropped, smoked, eaten, drunk, and injected most naturally occurring substances in an attempt to do just that.

In recent years we've abandoned the natural and turned to designer drugs to achieve the same ends. Unfortunately, drugs don't necessarily take you where you want to go and have a nasty habit of leaving you there. Emotional drugs are even more tempting. People work too many hours, talk too much, dedicate too many hours to the television, and obsess over their children, all in the name of seeking a better way to live, a better kind of human being to be.

Perhaps it is time to return to our rituals. Those that stay in mind for me are the biggies: Thanksgiving, Christmas, and Easter. Two of the three are based in the predominant religion of our culture and, though my family was not Christian, we observed the holidays with turkeys, trees, and painted eggs. The rolling around of our years was therefore landmarked by the church calendar.

In America, our rituals have eroded, holidays moved or commercialized beyond recognition. What remains is often sabotaged by those of us who don't want to work hard to keep the old ways or who have been so soured by Christmases past we no longer want to get our expectations up and fall into a funk over the holidays. We abandon tree and home and hide out in the Bahamas or go to work on Christmas Day. Often we feel the spirit of the holiday has abandoned us, and we turn away from the unsatisfying act of going through the motions.

In this, the second (and last) half of my life, I've felt a strong need to find ritual again. The feminist backlash against the white male religions (a backlash well earned; the place of women in the Bible is pretty doggone feeble) brought forth the earth mother then the witchy girl-power things popular in the seventies and eighties. These were deeply tempting but didn't work for me, not in the sense of bringing me closer to a spiritual life. They couldn't do what a combination of Mom's mashed potatoes and a couple verses of "Silent Night" could.

Apparently rituals need tradition, history to gather magic. They cannot be invented from whole cloth but must *become* from the needs of people. Spontaneous or incremental naturally occurring phenomena which are woven into the fabric of the brain when you are small enough not to reject them because of their seeming irrelevancy to daily life and personal success. For a ritual to be meaningful, it seems it must function as a bond between today and yesterday, between people now and the history that made us who we are. In connecting with our past through ritual, we anchor ourselves, connect with others of our culture past and present, become more whole, stronger, freer, able to venture out of our safe houses and into the unknowable house of our God.

Without traditions, our ritualistic connection to our past and the gods of our past, there can occur a lonely sense of just being a speck on the crust of the earth, belonging nowhere, having no meaning other than a blip on life's radar. On my darker days I believe this blip to be the sum total of human existence.

In fact, one of the reasons I chose to believe in God was because meaninglessness was an unpleasant way to live. To be a part of tradition, to seek God through ritual as well as meditation and prayer, gives me a sense of connection. If I am connected, a part of some greater whole, then I am by definition meaningful. Though a toenail may be a small and humble part of the body, it is necessary to the overall comfort of the body. Ritual, tradition, allows me at least toenail status in life.

Finding my place in this did not come easily. I returned to a sense of comfort with, and joy in, tradition through embracing ritual. In my case, the Christian rituals as they are celebrated in the Episcopal church.

In the beginning, repetitions of prayers, movement, bowing when the cross passes the pew, and Communion were done strictly by my body, my soul and mind still firmly fixed on what I would have for lunch or if the dress I was wearing was too short for church. Over time, my body came to inform my mind. When I bowed to the cross, I thought of and prayed for humility. Taking the Communion bread and wine, I thought of and prayed for strength. Repeating the Apostles' Creed, I looked for what those declarations meant in my life.

After some years of this practice, meaning began to seep in around the edges of my daily chores. I became invested in my community, in my spiritual connection with others and the universe. From this was born an interest in finding the traditions of my past—both my personal past and the past of "my people."

Finally, through ritual and tradition, I learned to care. When I felt I was no longer an outsider but a member of a clan, a species, a tradition, I couldn't help but be concerned for those who had, in a very real way, become brothers and sisters to me. Caring in its myriad forms gives my life meaning. Whether that meaning will outlive this body is of no relevance. For now I can live with pride and sense of purpose.

vanity

Vanity is inescapable in our society. How one looks is the focus of the media, from glossy magazines which chronically obsess on thinner thighs and longer-lasting lipstick to the most respected news people who continue to describe female subjects by age and looks—grandmother of two, attractive brunette, petite redhead—even when covering serious stories.

The rewards for being pretty are enormous. Pretty people earn more, have more friends, get called on more often in class and, yes, even get better grades. Life's treats are handed out to pretty people. Ugly people have to earn them. Add to the mix that, in America, pretty equals young, and it is no surprise plastic surgery is a booming industry.

My love affair with the mirror began my second year in high school. Till then I'd been a grubby little country kid riding bikes and building stickerweed forts. I know I must have been aware of my looks and cared in some rudimentary way—I remember the thrill of ordering new school clothes from the Montgomery Ward catalogue each August—but I have no recollection of staring into mirrors, checking hair, face, hemlines, butt width, tummy protrusion.

Mom was an anomaly in the fifties. A pilot, a woman in a man's world, she wore Levis, tennis shoes (I haven't see her in a dress more than a handful of times my whole life), no makeup and, since she was born blessed with thick, naturally curly red hair, she never wore curlers or owned a hair dryer. In our house, all it took to be "pretty" was to run a comb through your hair and wash your hands and face.

In high school this grand obliviousness was blasted away. It took very little time before I was made aware of the tremendous advantages the pretty had over the ugly or even the merely plain. And a little scrubbing and combing wasn't sufficient to the task. Since I dormed with twenty-four other adolescent girls, I quickly learned how to make my fairly decent face and okay hair into prettiness through the fine arts of plucking, primping, and painting. Pain was no obstacle. Men often wonder why women have such a high tolerance for pain; the agonies of giving birth are often touted. Not so, at least for my generation. Sleeping on jumbo brush rollers is what did it: girdles and very pointed shoes, eyelash curlers, pegged Levis, and combing out teased and sprayed hair. The United States Marines have nothing on the girls of the fifties and sixties.

The results of my efforts in these directions was amazing. By the end of my sophomore year I was a member in good standing of the In Crowd, going steady with the captain of the basketball team, and firmly on my way toward a life of glancing at my reflection in store windows and endlessly "growing my hair out."

Since I subsequently chose the theater as my profession, there was never a time during my twenties and thirties when looks ceased to matter so much. Vanity went from a pastime to a necessity. Actors work or don't, depending on their looks. For men, there is a wide range of looks that are considered handsome and, for those who don't fit, there are always character roles and villains. For women, the definition of pretty is brutally narrow and even the villianesses must fit into it.

Perhaps because, though never beautiful, with effort I could attain a good solid pretty, I enjoyed the trappings of fashion and vanity. I liked getting my hair cut and foiled, trying on clothes, wearing makeup. I even enjoyed, as the Chenille Sisters so aptly phrased it, wearing "high-heeled, pointy-toed girl's shoes."

Because I took pleasure in maintaining my vanity, it wasn't until my late thirties that I became aware of its weight, of the burden it was to tend so assiduously to one's looks.

Two things happened that changed my perspective. One was the inevitability of gravity overcoming elasticity. I was aging and, for women, and most especially for women who make their bread and butter by standing in front of a camera, age is the enemy, bringing a loss of status, a diminishing of choices, a drop in the number of job offers.

The other event was more sudden and revelatory. By my late thirties, though I still made my living as an actor in the Twin Cities in Minnesota, I'd taken to spending my summers as a seasonal ranger in the National Parks. The year I turned thirty-eight, I was sent on my first wildfire, serving as an emergency medical technician. For twenty-one days I lived in northern Idaho in a tent in a remote fire camp, showering in the trailer of a semi truck fitted up for the purpose and brushing my teeth at the communal outdoor sinks. Everybody wore the olive-drab and lemon-yellow fire-retardant clothes. Everybody wore heavy leather boots. Everybody stank of smoke and sweat.

And there were no mirrors. None. The only thing that could possibly pass muster as such was the polished strip of aluminum over the sinks used by the men for shaving. In this democratic surface everyone looked more or less the same: a smooth blob with smudges for eyes.

For three weeks I did not see myself, not so much as a glimpse of my reflection in a plate-glass window. For the first few days I was grateful, because I knew I must look like hell. Then, well, I just sort of forgot to care. I was just me, on the earth, laughing, talking, bandaging blistered feet, cleaning cuts and scrapes. There was just one of me, whole and happy inside a good strong body that did what I required of it. The second me, the part of the ego that slipped out of my body every time I looked in a mirror to peer back at me from reflected eyes passing judgment and making demands, had vanished along with the looking glass.

When I became aware of this phenomenon (as opposed to merely experiencing it), I realized what a drag vanity, both personal and professional, had become. The image in the mirror was a nag, a pest, a haint always pulling me out of life to criticize, adjust, or compliment the thin layer of skin and hair draped over my skull. To be without this badgering female was like quiet after racket, solitude after crowds.

At length, early snows put the fires out, the camp was demobilized, and we were all sent home.

The revelation of what life was like without vanity stayed strong for nearly a month before it began to fade and the judge waiting over the bathroom sink returned to direct my life.

I still loved pretty dresses and silly shoes. I spent too much money on cosmetics and enjoyed each and every new lipstick shade but, as I turned fifty, the nag in the mirror became ever more critical of what time was doing to my face and seldom was she totally satisfied with my attempts to hide the evidence. Some mornings, if I'd had a bad night's sleep, she could be downright bitchy.

After one such unpleasant exchange, I found myself before the computer clicking through the before-and-after pictures on the plastic surgery sites. Confidence undermined, I heard myself telling my husband: "I just don't look like Me anymore."

The pathos of that comment stuck in my mental craw. (Now there's an unsettling image . . .) Questions of "Me" and what "Me" looked like floated around my brain. The mirror, the nag, the critic, the judge told me I didn't look like Me anymore. She insisted Me wasn't a day over thirty-five and had little or no gray in her hair. That was Me. This sagging creature, hair shot with streaks of white, wrinkles from laughing and crying and staring at the sun too much dwarfing the feet of earthly crows, was someone else entirely.

My husband and my dogs still recognized me. Friends still said hello when they met me on the street. Happily encased in a healthy body, I still *felt* like myself. My livelihood no longer depended on taut skin or the agelessness of my hair. Though I do enjoy attention, the thought of attracting boys who make passes generates nothing in my heart but minor amusement and vague alarm. The way I look now serves now's purposes better than would the face the nag thinks I should fight to keep. This earned and weathered visage is comforting to children, soothing to traffic cops, and reassuring to loan officers.

If I cannot get this through the head of the nag in the mirror, if she continues to drag me out of life to serve at the feet of a vanity that is increasingly unrewarding, I have decided to banish her again. Or, better yet, like the Mad Woman of Chaillot, I shall replace her mirror with one of polished bronze and look at myself once each morning in this compassionate surface.

"Ah, there you are," I shall say. "How excellent to see you so alive."

betrayal

Not too long ago terrorists bombed the World Trade Center and the Pentagon. Along with millions of other Americans I watched the towers collapse and the lower end of Manhattan disappear in a cloud of smoke and debris. The Friendly Skies had been hijacked, our peace had been hijacked, and the hijackers, people we didn't know and who didn't know us, people who'd lived in our houses and eaten our food and enjoyed the good things this country has to offer, smashed these things into us, broke our bodies and burned our buildings.

Like so many others I was in a state of shock. I didn't know what to think. I didn't even know what I was feeling. The next day there was an evening service at my church. All day I waited for it, not knowing why I needed to go, really, but feeling that I did. I'd thought it was at 6:30 but, when I got there, it was nearly over. It had been scheduled for 6. I sat in the last row and, moments later, went up for Communion. The last song was played. The priest and the altar people recessed. The priest said the final benediction. As everyone rose to leave, I burst into tears. I did not cry like a grownup with sedate sniffles and dabs at the eyes with a tissue. Like a little kid I sobbed, great gulping wet sobs. In public. Even as I cried, a little part of me was observing, amazed, saying, "Now what the heck is *this* all about?"

It was about the total helpless, hopeless, childlike desperation one feels when betrayed; when the world you've come to rely on, even love, is brutally smashed, changed forever through no fault of your own. Things will never be the same; you will never be the same. An essential innocence has been destroyed.

In the wake of the bombings the nation was mobilized to go to war against terrorism, pledging to fight it regardless of cost. We were given the balm of action, of retribution. The villains were named, and we struck out against them. There was solace in this, not for our losses but for that helpless child within. In taking charge, setting out to destroy the enemy, a sense of purpose, dignity, and strength were restored.

Since this national tragedy, betrayal has been much on my mind. I have been considering betrayal that destroys not buildings and cities but nevertheless is incredibly destructive to our lives.

In the past half century, I have been betrayed a number of times and, much worse, I have been the betrayer an equal number. Of all the colors in my motley past, betrayal is the blackest. Betrayal is epidemic: married people cheat, priests betray congregations, parents molest children, policemen take bribes, the president lies. Sometimes the very people we have been taught to trust and rely on cannot be trusted or relied on.

When we are betrayed on this personal level, against whom do we declare war? In order to betray, one must first befriend, make promises to be broken, create expectations that are not met. I was betrayed by those closest to me, and I betrayed those who loved me most. That's the nature of the game. So against whom can war be declared? The straying spouse, the lying brother-in-law, the two-faced friend? Even in our overweening need to get past the hurt, to find the anger and strike out so we can feel in control again, safe, vindicated, most of us are aware that the consequences of our acts would be as damaging as the betrayal itself.

In a war against terrorism, there's the hope that in catching and punishing the terrorists, they can be stopped from further acts of violence. On a personal level, there is no hope of that, or slim hope. Will attack stop the cheating husband? Change the two-faced friend? People seldom alter their behaviors until they choose to. Short of murder, we have to accept the fact that we will not stop them. And, indeed, their evil may have been only against us. When that is known, our desire is unmasked for what it is: not an act for the good of society but old-fashioned revenge.

When I was first betrayed badly it was by the impersonal auspices of the theater. I had given my all to the theater. I had studied and worked and auditioned, and yet I was failing. Because I'd put my self-worth into my work, when the theater ignored me I felt betrayed, as if the entity were a person. My first instinct was to respond like a child—or perhaps a girl raised on movies and books where, if you suffered deeply enough, Prince Charming, John Wayne, or Dad would bail you out. So I suffered. Oddly enough, "the theater" didn't care one little bit. In the need to find some sort of logic, control, I declared war on myself. I felt betrayed, therefore I must have done something heinous. Much the reaction of an abused child or a battered wife.

The next few betrayals came pretty much all in a bunch, one after another for seven years. These were the worst kind, not by a centerless concept but by real live people. The first time I declared war. In crippling them, I crippled myself. When it was my turn and I was the betrayer, the person I'd hurt struck back till we were both in pieces. The third time—my turn again to be the victim—I declared war on myself and landed in a hospital for five weeks for severe depression.

On the interpersonal level, regarding emotional betrayals rather than criminal acts, there seemed to be no end to the helplessness, no solution to the pain, no way to regain the sense of safety. War against others or myself was not the answer.

During the healing years, betrayal was something I came to respect deeply about the Christian symbol of Christ on the cross.

It is primitive, inhumane, gory, macabre, even, as my mother has said, ghoulish. There is just no pretty way to depict a human being stripped, nailed, and lashed to a pair of timbers, beaten, stabbed, mocked, and left to die in front of his mother and his friends. It is the very essence of personal betrayal, betrayal taken to its end: not merely death but the destruction of a life.

Yet, according to the stories of the man, Jesus did not try in any way to make war on His attackers. Not on Judas who sold Him, Peter who denied Him, or any of the others who stood and watched as He was hauled away and who were too cowardly to even come keep Him company on Calvary. Jesus plotted no revenge nor dreamed of any. No threats were made to tattle to God and bring down His wrath. In fact, the story tells first of understanding, then forgiveness, then resurrection. The only individual who did not survive the crucifixion a resurrected man was Judas, and it was by his own hand.

In the story of this ignoble, sordid, ugly death of the carpenter's boy, I saw the ultimate betrayal, and I was shown a way out of the sewer of self-and-other-hatred in which my betrayals and the betrayals of others had landed me. It wasn't forgiveness that I was able to identify with. And only now am I beginning to understand forgiveness of self. It was the acceptance.

Jesus took the hit. Held the anger and the sorrow and the pain without any attempt to avoid it or hurl it back at those who had injured Him. He endured it, and ultimately He was freed, brought to a new and better life.

That's what I taught myself to do. I admit I whine a whole lot more than Jesus of Nazareth did and for a whole lot less reason, but I am better now at taking the hit, holding the pain and moving on. By taking the pain and finding room for it as I would the pain of a toothache, I have not cured or escaped the consequences of the injury, but at least I have contained it. It's as if betrayal is acid. In warring, throwing it out again to revenge myself on others, the burning went on and on. Each hurt spawned retaliatory hurts until the initial betrayal spun itself into a web of hate that touched many people the way a war inevitably kills the innocent along with the guilty. In holding the acid within, I have only the consolation of knowing I have not added to the world's angst. Perhaps in doing so I have lessened the hurt not only for others, but for myself.

The next step in the lesson of the cross is forgiveness. That's a bit harder but, when I've been able to truly achieve it, the burden of the acid is lifted from me. When I can manage that, the resurrection comes as the symbol the crucified Christ promises. I emerge new-born and stronger into a better life.

My beloved ex-mother-in-law was fond of saying, "That which does not kill us makes us strong." To that I add: "In forgiving that which does not kill us we are made strong again."

an argument for life after death

Yesterday I went to the funeral of a baby. My friend's nine-day-old granddaughter had died of SIDS. The funeral was at 11:30, the visitation at 10:30. I asked Joan, who accompanied me, if a visitation was the same as a viewing, because I wasn't all that keen on seeing a dead baby. Joan said she thought it was just a time to tell the bereaved you thought enough of them and their bereavement to come and grieve with them, that you were sorry for the pain they were experiencing, and that usually infants aren't given the open-casket treatment.

We arrived at the funeral parlor—or I guess I should say "home," as "parlor" seems to have gone out of fashion—between ten-thirty and eleven. The place was so crowded we had to park out back. This tiny scrap of a baby would be missed by a lot of people. Parents, grandparents, friends, all had been invested on one level or another with this new spark of life in the world.

We were directed upstairs. Joan led us through clusters of people talking, weeping, or just looking confused and vaguely concerned. In the face of death, many—including myself—were ill at ease, uncomfortable with our thoughts. The crowd grew thicker as we neared the center of this gathering.

The center was actually a dead end. I assume this was the fault of the funeral home's designers, who'd not mastered the concept of crowd flow.

I followed Joan into a room, scarcely eight feet on a side, where we saw Polly and Martha. Needing a place to roost, I joined them. Joan disappeared, the tail of her cream and black skirt flicking out of sight into a pod of drab-suited men.

"Where's Emily?" I asked. Emily was who I came for, my friend, and the grandmother of the baby.

"Just in there," Martha told me.

Past the thick backs of the suited men was another doorway. There were not that many people between me and it but, because the room was so tight, we felt and moved like a crowd. I started toward the beefy wall as Joan eeled back through and laid a hand on my arm.

"Is Emily in there?"

"Yes," she told me. "So is the baby."

The dead baby.

"Okay," I said. "I've got to look." Why? I don't know. Because it was there. Because I had to.

I may not have gone through with it, but Emily met me. I hugged her, was inarticulate, inappropriate, and awkward as I often am when faced with saying something for which no words are adequate.

She thanks me for coming. Takes my arm and walks me into the last and smallest room. Murmurs around us: "So sweet. Just like she's sleeping." Tears. Makeup running, leaving mascara tracks.

People part because I am arm in arm with Family. At the back wall of the airless, windowless, shrinking room is a tiny white coffin. White fabric froths from within. Nestled in the lace and satin is a baby. Only the face and hands show.

Not sleeping. Dead. Totally dead.

Perhaps this last viewing comforts the family. If so, I am all for it. To me, it's grotesque. Weird. Upsetting. I feel desperate and strange.

I turn my back on the coffin, say inane things I don't remember to Emily, and flee.

Needless to say, I spent a good part of the rest of the day wondering why the baby didn't look as if she were sleeping, what essential thing had gone.

I have seen some dead people. One was killed by violence, shot in the head while fleeing the police through the Los Angeles bus terminal. One was a derelict dead on the street in Manhattan. One a young man smashed in a car crash. Three dead in the National Parks, all of heart attacks.

The man in bus station and the derelict I didn't get close to. The others I saw in my job as a park ranger. My work then was to keep air going into their lungs and their hearts pumping till they reached the hospital where others would declare enough was enough and life had gone.

The only real moment of death I have witnessed up close and personal was when my husband and I finally made the decision to have his old and crippled corgi, Miss Tilly, put "to sleep."

Not wanting Miss Tilly to feel alone or afraid, I held her, kept eye contact as the veterinarian administered the shot. I saw the life leave Tilly's eyes. It was her right eye, that liquid brown that makes us love and trust dogs. She was looking up at me, and then she was gone. It didn't look as if she'd gone to sleep; it was crystal clear that the essential Tillyness went away. All that remained was a furry inanimate thing, like a doll made to look like Miss Tilly.

Because I watched an old sick dog die and then pondered the corpse of an infant girl, I came to believe in life after death. I could see life; it was something, a real thing, not merely an animation of matter. I saw it, and then I saw it leave.

It concerns me not at all that we transplant organs, clone, and fiddle with DNA. We simply cannot touch life, that light, spark, bit of eternity, splinter of God. We who *are* life don't even know what it is. I haven't the faintest idea where it goes, nor do I pretend to know where it comes from, but now I do know that it *is*. It passes through this mortal coil, but we do not create it. And we cannot destroy it.

What once made that baby more than the sad crumpled thing in the coffin didn't end. It went someplace else.

This isn't much comfort to the living because we, with a natural and healthy joy, deeply love life—at least those of us who are not too broken inside. The life in that little girl, in Miss Tilly, made us celebrate on a moment-to-moment basis, on a level so intimate that it continued under anger, sickness, disappointment. When that spark near which we warm our souls leaves, we mourn.

In the hours following the funeral, I knew the value of life, all life, everybody's life. I saw it glittering all around me. I know this knowledge will come and go, and I will mourn every time I lose sight of one beloved speck of it.

For reasons I cannot quite explain, I now know it is not destroyed and, one day, the shining in my eyes will dim as my life passes, and I will find out where we go from here.

things

When I was a young woman it was the fashion to eschew material things. We prided ourselves on our pseudo-poverty and called home when we needed money for tuition.

Because I chose a life in the arts, until I was in my forties, I remained among the genteel poor, the poor-by-choice who never missed a meal and considered the lack of a color TV a sign of moral superiority.

Finally my books began to sell, and at last there was money with which to buy things. Now I delight in them. I love my pretty dresses and shiny shoes, my house, garden, my snazzy new bicycle and my adorable little Miata, trips to Europe and Nepal. I love my success: getting treats, meeting fancy people at posh events, speaking to crowds that have traveled from their homes to see me, to tell me that they admire me.

Maybe because this came later in life, I have no sense of entitlement, just tremendous pleasure and the knowledge that I am blessed, that the gift of storytelling that was given to me is of value to others.

This wealth of things brought back to me the words of my aunt Peg, a school teacher in Babylon, New York, with whom I was arguing the liberal hippie philosophy (somewhere between anarchy and the potlatch). Aunt Peg, a Republican, said to my twenty-one-year-old self, "Of course you're not conservative. *You* have nothing to conserve."

Now I have much to conserve. I find myself voting for tax cuts instead of education and other mental phenomena that continue to surprise or embarrass me.

I have also noted a mild sense of anxiety that rears its head from time to time that there may come a day when I will no longer be able to afford all this stuff. This was made more real to me when President Bush declared war on terrorism.

News of the attack itself shifted over to news of nationwide changes and privations resulting not from Ground Zero but from our reaction to Ground Zero. Terrorism was spreading from the deed of the terrorists to the first terrors of a country at war. Word came of airlines cutting flights, laying off pilots, going out of business.

My sister is a retired airline pilot. Should her carrier go bankrupt, what becomes of her pension? The Federal Aviation Agency grounded even small planes. My parents used to manage a little mountain airport in northern California. I know the shoestring many small operators run on. How many families will lose their livelihood?

The ever-widening ripples must eventually affect my own comfortable sphere. People may have less money to buy books or less inclination to read. Perhaps they will want a new kind of book, not the murder mysteries that I write but something more soothing—or more vengeful.

The golden era that I've had the great good fortune to live in could very well be coming to an end.

I could lose my stuff.

As a child and a young woman, I had little in the way of things—jobs, money, status—and I was obnoxiously happy. In early middle age, the "things" began to roll in. Whatever I wished for, I got. At that time I would think: "If only I could get this . . ." or: "If only that would happen . . ." I would be happy. I got this and that and remained miserable. These past few years I have been given all the things, and I am happy.

Clearly, once basic needs are met, happiness is not dependent on things. This is obviously not an original thought or stunning revelation. Most of us pay lip service to it; we know money can't buy happiness, but few of us really believe it. If we did, we wouldn't fuss so about getting and keeping and storing and polishing and buying and selling and finally bequeathing our things.

My personal retrospective on "things" was a heartening departure from my usual pattern. In reviewing a life of things and no-things in view of moving from the former to the latter, I realized, much as I love my luxuries, I have invested remarkably little of my self-worth in them. I have not come to think my life would be of less value without them. Though I would sorely miss cable TV, salon haircuts, and ten thousand other little treats, I would not necessarily be unhappy should they vanish.

In realizing this, it occurred to me that I've been praying all wrong lo these many years. Part of my daily prayers, as well as the ritual prayers at the Episcopal church I attend, involve thanking God for my things: the roof over my head, the food on my table, my good health, a wonderful hiking trip through the Alps, my dogs and cats.

With the exception of my dogs and cats, God—or whatever one chooses to call the higher power—gave me none of it. People gave those things to me. All of them; from the upbringing and education that led me to be a writer right on down to the genes that allow me good health.

Not a single job, dollar, dress, or trip did God give me.

Awareness of this cleared up a whole passel of mysteries, anomalies, and apparent contradictions where God is concerned, questions along the line of why God would give a child molester perfect health and a good mother ovarian cancer; why He bestows wealth on a godless football player and a faithless wife on a good Christian minister.

The answer is, obviously, He doesn't. People, fate, luck,

genetics—the things of the world—cause these uneven transpirations.

What God gave me had nothing whatsoever to do with *things,* with money, respect, or attention. What God gave me through knowing Him—on a wordless, instinctual level when I was young and on the conscious, thinking level during the past handful of years—is the *ability* to be happy regardless of the ebb and flow of the *things* of the world. The decade I blocked Him out with anger, lust, addiction, and arrogance, though I continued to possess the miraculous spark of life that is the soul, I was unable to be happy because I lacked a connection to something greater than myself. Corporeal successes and three-dimensional goods failed to alleviate my gloom. Now, with a sense of the divine lodged somewhere behind my breastbone, I have the ability to feel joy. Joy not only in the goodies of this life but, should they cease to be, joy in what remains and, most especially, joy in the lives that touch mine.

If one should choose to be Jesuitical about this, a dozen questions jump to mind: are the unhappy the ungodly? The joyful monster godly? Sorry. I can't answer those. I have only one woman's experience of one life half lived. For me, God gives the things of God: life, love, the ability to feel joy and compassion. The ability to feel sorrow and pain is the darker side of the gift but, because these are the things of God, seeking God through them and about them bears fruit.

For everything else I suggest seeking a good investment counselor.

sex

Harrumph, sheesh, and egad! The national bugaboo and/or obsession—depending on who you ask and what year it is when you ask it—is with sex. Till I was sixteen, it was talked about too little, then it was done too much, now it's talked about too much and in all the wrong ways. We've gone from a nation of puritans to a nation of adolescents struggling to find a way through MTV and Hollywood to some sort of truce with our natural reproductive urges. And all this without a sense of true connection. How could people get something as natural and necessary as eating or breathing so terribly muddled?

My entire sex education (taking place in the sixties) consisted of one sentence uttered with firmness and embarrassment by my father: "Sex is a wonderful thing for *married* people." "Married" was stressed in hopes I would not become one of the missing; the girls who simply vanished from high school one day, never to be seen again, and talked about only in frightened whispers.

The next installment of my education came from a film shown in the mid-sixties by the Sisters of Mercy at Mercy High School. In this memorable docudrama, Phoebe, a teenage girl, has short and sordid sex with her boyfriend. Phoebe gets pregnant. The last glimpse of the boyfriend is of the taillights of his car disappearing into a rainy night as he hastily leaves town. Phoebe then kills herself. And let that be a lesson to you girls!

Many of us didn't know what went where, or what one did with one's nose when kissing. We were told we'd go to hell for any use of tongues. French-kissing was deemed a mortal sin along with murder and adultery.

Clearly options were limited and costs dear.

We were given no information, no rationale, no logic, or understanding of the reasoning behind retaining one's virginity. Only a terrible fear of the consequences should we lose it prior to matrimony. That terrifying prospect might have kept our virtue intact but for the entrance of cheap, reliable, available birth control on the market. It's possible a Catholic upbringing kept the girls of my acquaintance on the straight and narrow (though I have serious doubts about that), but I was not Catholic. I'd attended Mercy High not for the religious instruction but because it was the only top-notch high school my parents could afford. I was a heathen; I scoffed at mortal sin.

I went off to college and ran face-first into the sexual revolution. At the time, it was deemed heady stuff. I thought it was heady stuff. Looking back, I wonder at what alchemy, what undercurrent allowed the revolution to take the turn it did. Near as I can tell from what I remember and what I've gleaned of others' recollections of the times, we chose to let sexual mores, requirements, and pressures be dictated by boys in their teens and twenties. Is it any wonder the rules became more, sooner, faster, anytime, anywhere?

Maybe because we girls were so terribly naïve or maybe because, along with sex, war, drugs, and rock and roll, women's liberation was in the wind, we thought to be equal to men was to be like men. And almost overnight, sex went from something we were protected from to something we sensed we had to do to buy a place on the glorious front lines. Not that it was thought of that way. We would have sworn we did our own thinking. If thinking was involved, it was done by young people with no real experience of life based on what others as ignorant and arrogant as ourselves said was true and right and good.

Herpes, AIDS, abortions, the end of the war in Vietnam or, more likely, the growing up of the ersatz soldiers ended the revolution. Some good had been achieved: cats out of the bag, tolerance, less fear and secrecy. The greatest good had to do with the control of women's bodies by the women who dwelt within them and the choice of when and if to have children.

Still the sexual revolution, like many a bloodier fight, left a dark legacy, and some of its rank and file were among the walking wounded. We had had lots of sex but were no closer to any kind of understanding about what it could be. The pressure not to have sex had merely been replaced with the pressure to have sex. Nowhere in the mix was there a place for the natural growth and sensitivities of girls and young women. We had, once again, subjugated our needs to the needs of boys and men. Now we felt the pressure to view sex as men viewed it. Or, more accurately, how we perceived they viewed it.

From the repression of the fifties we have traveled into oversaturation. Now sex is not only talked about openly, it is unavoidable. Movies cram sex scenes—most unrealistic, many violent—into the most unlikely places. It's as if a movie must have a sex scene regardless of the needs of the plot or characterization. Because of the Internet, pornography is enjoying a wider audience. And pornography, whether one approves or disapproves, does not address the needs of girls and young women. It is not made for girls and young women. It steadfastly pours images into the minds of men and boys in which the idiosyncratic needs of women simply do not exist. Perhaps that is its greatest allure: sex without regard for others, selfish sex for the gratification of one. Ads, television, magazines—all are inundated with strong sexual messages. Most seem to suggest that wild, irresponsible, transporting sex is being had by everybody all the time. Those that are serious talk about disease and unwanted pregnancies. Nowhere is there the discussion of the meaning of sex, why it's complex for us; who we are as sexual beings. Or even, other than babies and lusts, why we have sex at all.

You may note (as I just did) that in this piece I have referred to a vague "we" rather than the "I" of personal experience. Despite the pictures, films, and words about sex that inundate our society, it's still embarrassing to speak of it on a personal level. What if my experience is wrong? Unusual? Will I be seen as repressed, "square"—words used by men to pressure me into sex when I was young?

I guess, as a woman of supposed courage, I must delve into the personal if there's to be anything to this essay other than a narrow retrospective of Sex in Our Times.

As I was shifting from my teens to my twenties, the changing pressures to not have, then to have, sex, put the sexual act outside for me, outside of my Self. There was no time, no guidance provided, no quarter given, for me to grow into my own sexuality in my own time and my own way by coming to know my own body or my psychological needs. I was rushed and hurried into the act armed not with what I thought or wanted but only with what I thought I was supposed to think or want. Mostly that was what men thought or wanted. To be "cool," to be equal, was to approach sex as I was taught a man would. In our Victorian past, men, desiring sex, were showing their baser natures. Women, refusing, were exhibiting virtue. That changed abruptly to men, in desiring, were being natural and free; women, in refusing, were exhibiting frigidity and repression. Both are wrong, but at least the Victorians admitted that men and women think differently about sex. This was impossible for me to admit till I was well into my thirties. I believed the only hope of equality was in vehemently proclaiming that the only difference between the genders was their plumbing.

James Stevenson, a friend of mine in Minneapolis, once told me that as a young man enjoying a misspent youth, he'd believed women and men viewed sex the same way. When he was rejected, it couldn't really be because the women didn't *want* sex, therefore they must be messing with his mind. When he realized (after marrying a truly splendid woman) that this was not so, he wanted to call every woman he'd ever pressured and apologize. What stopped him, he said, was the fear that they'd say: "Stevenson . . . Stevenson? No . . . I don't remember any Stevenson. . . ."

The result of the combined weirdness of the times and my own psyche was to leave me with three unspoken and, till I'd grown far enough from them to have some perspective, unexamined tenets regarding sex.

First was a sense of power and exaggerated importance. I had the power to give or withhold something that was desirable. I could use the vague promise of the prize to manipulate men.

Second was a sense of danger. In my person, I carried a treasure that men were willing to commit violence and/or deceit to wrest from me.

Third was a sense of being hounded. That because I was the

keeper of the cookie jar, men were constantly harassing me to share something I might not wish to share. Guilt was often the result of refusing. When I came to have committed relationships, I would feel a terrible guilt when I chose not to have sex.

I don't know which of these three emotions did the most damage, but the combination was potent: power led to fear and guilt, creating a toxic mess where joy and connection should have been growing.

Most of my forties was spent unraveling the tangle. Through therapy, meditation, writing, and long conversations with my sister and my women friends, I re-created an early sex education for myself, an education that stressed the emotional aspects of the act, not the physical. Decades after the doomed Phoebe killed herself, there are still few, if any, guidelines to go by. Because I had long thought of sex as something outside of myself over which I had control only at great personal cost, I had to go back to the beginning and try to recapture sexuality as part of myself, find out what the experience meant to me in a basic way and what I wanted from it.

Since I do not live in a vacuum and good sex requires two people with different needs meeting on the same plane, my search required total and unremittingly supportive cooperation from my husband, which I was fortunate enough to get. As my quest required several months of complete abstinence to clear the decks, clean the palate, and rewind old tapes, his loving contribution cannot be underestimated.

Now hovering around the Age of Wisdom at the half-century

mark, I am more or less at peace with my sexuality. I have found that place where the body and the spirit mesh when two people come together.

Sometimes I resent having had to make this journey at all and having had to make it without guidance. Now I look around at the movies, the ads, and I wonder what our girls will be taught, if there is any place in these battering images and demands where they can find a comfortable safe place to grow into their bodies, find their connections. I doubt it. In thinking about the naturalness of sex, I'd often compared it to eating: something necessary and pleasurable and, above all, natural. But even eating has become unnatural. Our foods are fast and fatty, our girls shown razor-thin women after whom to model themselves, then bombarded with food till they grow fat (or perceive themselves as fat) and begin the futile cycle of dieting and binging.

As I have worked on this book, I've tried to avoid presenting problems with no solutions, problems for which I cannot suggest at least a ray of light at the end of the tunnel. I'm afraid this is such a piece. I wish I had a solution. I wish I knew what I could say to young girls that would counteract the poisons of the media and peer-group pressure. Unfortunately, just at the time our girls could use this guidance, they are separating from their elders, moving into a society of peers. It's a time when they can no longer hear us.

Our daughters need support groups populated not only with the young but with the matrons, the spinster aunties, the crones. There is no time in our hurried world, fragmented into nuclear families, for the gentle nurturing only women can give to girls moving into adulthood. The village, the extended families with aunts and cousins and grandmothers available when moms don't have all the answers, is gone. Because we have scoffed at our elders for so long, now that we are the elders, our children cringe when advice is offered and cannot hear our words or accept our truths. Perhaps the only hope is that we, regardless of age or marital status, can only seek to find our own sexuality, our own peace, and hope to influence by example.

Child-development folks—at least most of them—are now suggesting that children learn a lot of their behaviors, reactions, and fears and develop key personality traits when they are very young. More than any other factors, these ways of viewing life are formed by parents or primary caretakers. When discussing children as young as this, in most instances, one can't say they've learned from any sort of formal lessons. There's a technical term for it, I'm sure, but here I'll simply use "osmosis." Children seem to pick things up from us by osmosis. Who we really are, our innermost fears and fusses, show up on their little radar screens, and they drink it in because, despite what we say, what they feel is our truth.

In my perfect world, the women's groups in which we find such sustenance would extend membership privileges to our girl children. They would be a place they could hear the talk of women, have their questions answered, find sanctuary, be unafraid and unashamed.

Since this doesn't seem to be in the offing, at least not any time soon, maybe there is hope in just finding security and peace with our gender and our sexuality from recreation to recreation. Know who we are and what we want and what we don't and be at home with that.

Perhaps when we are no longer afraid or ashamed, when we have a strong and working sense of our own sexuality, it will trickle down to our daughters.

guilt

Guilt has got to be one of the most versatile emotions going. Not to mention one of the most abused. We use it to goad, punish, remind, torture, teach, motivate, and pay off old debts. Most of the people I know carry loads of guilt that, if turned into cotton balls, would stagger a strong camel. I carry guilt from things I did when I was six and ten, fourteen, thirty-six, forty-five. There seems to be no statute of limitations on guilt, and it has a greater half-life than unrequited love. Erma Bombeck put it perfectly: "Guilt: the gift that keeps on giving."

Like pain, it is one of the necessary unpleasantnesses of life inasmuch as it exists to keep us from committing an act that will hurt others or us—sort of like swatting the dog with the newspaper when he gets into the garbage—a nasty reminder that what we have done is unacceptable.

How this handy device for the healthy evolution of the soul was turned into an epidemic of angst, I have no idea. So much of the guilt I suffer, that I see in those close enough to me to talk about such things, is not of this useful kind. It is suffering because we somehow feel we are responsible for things over which we have no control, and, even more so, suffering because we haven't the humility to accept with grace and goodness of heart that we are fallible.

A while back I added a sunroom onto my house. This was the first time I'd ever undertaken a building adventure that I couldn't do myself in the privacy of my garage. I didn't hire an architect because the builder told me this was such a simple structure I didn't need to waste the money. Well, as fate would have it, the promised simplicity was an illusion, and the architect would have been a most excellent addition to the team. I suffered guilt because *I should have known.* To relieve the pressure of this sensation, I talked to a friend who had once been a contractor. Then he suffered guilt because he *should have known.* So there was all this guilt clouding the good things of life because two perfectly nice people thought they should have been omniscient.

Skeeter, a cat of mine, was killed by a pack of dogs. I was on the back deck smoking a cigarette (hey, I never said I'd conquered all of my vile addictions), and I heard the cat screaming. It took me fifteen to twenty seconds to grasp that a cat was in trouble, another few to grab shoes, vault the fence, and run into the fray. I was too late. I rushed her to the vet, but she'd been so badly mauled she died the next day. The guilt was immense. *I should have known* what was happening sooner. I should have been faster. I should have gone without the shoes, without putting out the cigarette.

I expect, in reading this, you (if you are a good and compassionate soul) will have instantly "forgiven" me for not knowing what I had no experience or opportunity to know. Should you have told me these stories, I would not only have exonerated you for your guilt, but, had you persisted in suffering from it, actually grown impatient, wondering why you were being such an idiot.

Is this because we expect less of others than we do of ourselves? Or is it because in our egotism we believe we are better than others, that they can be forgiven because, unlike us, they are not so clever, so responsible, so strong and quick and all-seeing?

Where guilt is concerned, omniscience isn't all we expect of ourselves. I suffer guilt over saying the wrong thing without thinking, not picking up the tab at dinner quickly enough, talking too much, too little, being the life of the party, being the wallflower. The list is endless, and petty. I cannot even begin to touch on the littles of life we suffer guilt over, but it ranges from eating that extra brownie to feeling responsible because some distant ancestor, who lived according to the lights and mores of her time, didn't know it was inherently wrong to own slaves, kill buffalo, or burn witches.

Everything makes us feel guilty. Other people make us feel guilty. During my years (and years) of therapy, I was taught that no one can *make* me feel guilt, no one can *make* anyone else feel anything. So now I have to feel guilty about feeling guilty. What nonsense. To say no one can make us feel guilt is like saying Arnold Schwarzenegger cannot make us wince when we shake hands with him. Sure, if you're a spiritual Mr. Universe and can bench-press the equivalent of four hundred fifty pounds of emotional duress, you'll probably be okay. For the rest of us: guilt.

In contemplating this ubiquitous and odious sensation, I've come to the conclusion that most of the guilt we feel is either habit or egotism. The good, healthy kind of guilt, the kind that keeps us from touching that emotional hot plate again, is usually over quickly. The kind that lingers and dims our enjoyment of life is either learned and unquestioned or it can be accounted for by the simple fact that, like everybody else, we are flawed, works in progress. We don't think of all the ramifications every time we speak or act. We cannot see into the future. We cannot know everything. We make mistakes. And, still, we remain good people.

Most of the world's great religions tell us that we are made in God's image, that we are loved by God, and that God forgives us our sins. If this is taken literally, we must let God be the judge of our actions and not play judge and jury with an endless litany of guilts. If it's taken metaphorically, perhaps it is a way the sages let us know that to be an imperfect human is okay, that we can screw up—indeed, that we *will* screw up time and time again. That is the nature of our beast.

I've found only two cures for ambient guilt: self-examination and humility. If, when I examine the word or deed that brought on the spate of self-recrimination and find that I was not evil, not intending to hurt, but merely flawed in my ability to concentrate or know the unknowable, then I must check myself for hubris. I must see where it is that I fit into life. Is it in the pantheon of the all-powerful, all-seeing gods or is it down here in the rank and file of the blind leading the blind where I'm no brighter, no quicker, no cleverer, no kinder, no stronger than most? It's hard to do it, but sometimes I must accept that I am only human. When I do, I find I can cast off the chains. Or at least a few links.

the word

"Whoever said 'sticks and stones will break your bones but words will never hurt you' was an idiot." My Lutheran minister friend said that in one of his sermons, and it struck me with such a tremendous force of truth that I laughed out loud in church.

We have long known of the power of the word. We are told of, warned of, and reminded of this force throughout our history and culture. In the Christian Bible it says: "First there was the Word . . . and the Word was God." According to some interpretations of Genesis, the Word created the beings of the earth.

The magic of naming permeates our literature: Adam naming the creatures in the garden of Eden, the heroine needing to name Rumpelstiltskin to save her firstborn son. In *Tales of the Thousand and One Nights,* the right word could open doors: *Open, sesame.*

The pen is mightier than the sword. Our words both create and destroy. By what we choose to name and how we choose to name it we define one another, ourselves, our world and our gods. In naming, we create the truths that make up our day-to-day reality. If we say a snake is a fearful thing, and we say it often enough to ourselves and our children, when a snake appears the beholders are, in every real way, filled with fear.

J. M. Barrie captured this phenomena with a poetic simplicity that cuts to the heart: "Every time a child says, 'I don't believe in fairies,' somewhere there is a little fairy that falls down dead."

Our words bring emotions into being. They draw our beliefs from vague thoughts into concrete realities. They are of such importance that the words of our prophets, of Buddha, Muhammad, Jesus, Confucius, have been dissected for millennia. Scholars pluck up, turn about, and examine each and every word, searching for meaning, symbols, nuance. In our legal system, a person can die or be set free over the precise meaning of a word of law.

Regardless of this evidence of the power of the word in our lives, our beliefs, and our philosophies, we continue to behave as if this applies only to others. That the words *we* speak are not imbued with the same power but can be poured out thoughtlessly, as harmless as a breeze through the grass.

The phrase "created in God's image" has been variously interpreted to mean we look like God looks, are self-aware as God is self-aware, and are able to love as God is able to love. Perhaps another interpretation could be simply that we speak. We use words. We have the Word and with it the awful power of the word.

When I lie, I destroy the truth. When I say kind things, I engender kindness. When I spew words of anger and hatred, anger and hatred become living entities that reproduce both in my heart and mind and in those within range of my words. Words of fear frighten. Words of hope create hope. Words of despair crush hearts with despair.

This is not an esoteric concept if you think about it in mundane situations. Most of us have been content, happy until someone says an ugly word and our world is turned ugly. Maybe not forever, but for a minute or an hour or a day. We might admire an individual. A word is dropped in our ear and we no longer see that person in the same way.

I have been a profligate with my words; gossiping about someone I love till I feel my love sour as my unkind words make me unkind. I have used words to turn a hero into a fool, a savior into an opportunist, a god into a delusion, faith into shame.

Not only have I done this to others, I have done it to myself. I have turned my own words inward to change my innocence to stupidity, my vulnerability to weakness, my hope to foolishness. Using this same alchemy I've changed cruelty to strength, avarice to determination.

It was not till after I had written and spoken countless millions of words and sent them out into the world that I came to understand their power, my power.

Now I am more careful when I name things. Before I open the Pandora's box of my vocabulary I try to remember to look first for a kind, gentle, beautiful word with which to call a thing into being. I let the lie be a "mistake," the stupid be merely "ignorant," the mean simply "having a bad day." I have relearned something we all instinctively knew as children: once you name the thing that follows you home, it becomes more likely you will end up keeping it.

things that go bump in the night

There was no Halloween this year. Several things killed it. Because of the war on terrorism, the news channels have been having All-War-All-The-Time coverage twenty-four hours a day, seven days a week. The problem is there's only about an hour of newsworthy happenings. The other 167 hours need to be filled, so the talking heads use up the time with speculation and wild surmise regarding what *could* happen. They must keep it scary or we'll tune out and where will their ratings be? When Halloween rolled around this year, the "news" jumped on it and issued endless dire warnings about anthrax and other evils awaiting unwary children and urged parents to keep them home or send them to parties at the houses of trusted friends.

The other factor here in Mississippi was religion. A strong contingent of Christians in the Bible Belt have decided Halloween is tantamount to devil worship and do not allow their children to participate. Since Halloween fell on a Wednesday this year (a traditional church night in Dixie), the poor little buggers not only didn't get to trick-or-treat but were bundled off to the holy edifices instead. The children dressed as their favorite Bible characters and had an evening of holy fun. Very safe. Very pure. And missing the point entirely.

Halloween is a special night, a valuable night, especially for children. It's a night when, as a child, I became the thing that lived under my bed, in my closet. I remember the marvelous freedom of being out after dark—and sometimes on a *school night,* mind you—dressed as some wondrous beast or delightful fairy. Night crackled cool and electric on my skin. Houses and bushes grew larger with starlight, alive with wind but, for that one night, not scary. On Halloween, the ghosts and goblins that inhabited my nightmares were transformed by some ancient magic into children like myself. Darkness—usually frightening in my childish fancy—became mine, and I walked through it not as victim or prey but as landlord, owner. Children I saw every day at school metamorphosed into amazing creatures, out free and loose, to join in a conspiracy to lay siege to the forbidden.

Adults cowered indoors, only to peep out when we marched courageously up to their doors and issued the age-old blackmail threat: "Trick or treat?" Invariably, we were bought off with a treat, but there remained the delicious sense of power, knowing that, had they not paid the price, a trick could be played by us children on them, the adults, the Powers That Be in our short lives. I never played one single trick. But I knew I could have if I'd wanted to and, short of felonious matters, there would have been no consequences. Not on Halloween, not when I was free to be my monsters.

Ah, you might be thinking, but that was *then,* then when the world was safe. Not true. The world was no safer in the sixties when we took over the neighborhoods. Crime of every kind was higher then than it is now: assault, rape, kidnapping, molestation, murder. Even then there were urban legends to frighten our parents. Remember tales of razor blades in the apples? The difference was our parents had the good sense (or sufficient blissful ignorance) to scoff at apocryphal evils.

For reasons I don't understand, we, those selfsame trick-or-treaters of thirty and forty years ago, have allowed ourselves to be frightened into changing the lives of our children because we hear of something wicked happening thousands of miles away. It's drummed into us over the airwaves, and we respond as if it were happening right next door. We've become afraid of lawsuits, terrorists, being politically incorrect, offending, getting hurt, anthrax in candy apples, toxins in our water systems, lead in our paint, and *germs* on everything from toothbrush to toilet seat.

We *need* to be good. We're desperate to be safe.

And we are trying our damnedest to deny the side of us that

is not good, is not safe. Halloween is a night for meeting with our demons, but in disguise so they cannot get us. It celebrates our natural wildness, thirst for adventure and risk, our ability to imagine ourselves to be anything, to taste freedom from fear. To *be* the thing that jumps out at people from the dark, says outrageous things, growls and crows and hoots. This part of us is as valuable as the part that worships the light.

Arlo Guthrie once said: "You can't have a light without a dark to stick it in." Our goodness needs to have the creative input from the part of us that flirts with the unknown, challenges the status quo, braves the ogres. Without this, goodness becomes a fixed thing, regulated, stale and, finally, no longer goodness but merely obedience to rules we don't understand but adhere to out of fear of punishment.

Goodness is a living thing, it needs to be tested, rediscovered by each of us in our own way so we can find out how to best use our idiosyncratic abilities to serve others. Halloween traditionally was the night we were given the freedom to explore the dark—not to find and be the evil but to see that the night was as beautiful as the day, that we were powerful, others were kind, that there was candy behind those closed doors and strangers who gave us treats.

Being trusted to walk by ourselves in the world at night is an important ritual. That it comes but one day a year when we are small lets us discover this place, said to be inhabited by sinister forces, slowly and safely and by ourselves. On Halloween, we learn that we can meet with our demons; that monsters are really and truly just us in other guises; that we can survive this interface. We learn that we are trustworthy; that our parents can dress us as demons, send us out into the night of demons to move among the demons and yet trust us to do nothing worse than to beg candy off the neighbors.

When adult fears and conveniences take this world from us, herd us off to church and controlled environments, we learn that the world is indeed a horrifying place, that we are not safe in it, the demons are too much for us, neighbors offering candy are not above killing children, and we cannot to be trusted to roam even this one night a year without supervision.

Halloween is too necessary to consign to the ash heap of ancient wisdoms. It is the one night set aside for our children to confront evil on their own terms. For me, it was the night I learned evil was a construct of the mind and I need not be a part of it. Because of Halloween, I am free to walk alone in the dark.

children of god

Yesterday I had a revelation. Once again it happened to be while I was in church. The seeds of this were sown last Friday when I was prostrate with depression. (I know, I know, I've boasted previously of having conquered it, but there are still days . . .) I was lying on the sofa with my dogs watching *A History of God* on PBS. It was fascinating. Much of it I was familiar with from my eclectic and incomplete study of religions, but I'd never seen it laid out so lucidly.

The show worked its way forward from Abraham and his many gods to the movement among the Jews to worshipping one god, then to the advent of Jesus and the processing of His life into a smooth fit with the god of the Jews and monotheism. How in the decades after He died it was decided He was the son of God, then, many years after that that He was as divine as God. Next in this history was a council of church elders in Nicea, where the verbal and mental hijinks required to make this belief consistent with monotheism were enacted and, hence, the birth of the holy Trinity and, later, the addition to the Creed that Jesus was the *only* son of God. I admit to looking askance at the word-play that insists Christianity is not polytheism, when the language of the church and the New Testament continually separate Jesus from God by birth, responsibilities, temperament, and family ties, but this is the tricky construct chosen and codified at Nicea. The Nicene Creed is the one most Christians still espouse every Sunday.

During the tracing of this history something was mentioned that I'd known before but had slipped through the cracks of my mind. Jesus never said He was the only son of God. He referred to God as "Father." Thus, the seed of His godhood was planted to bloom several generations after His death.

Anyway, to get back to church on Sunday and my revelation.

As we knelt and Father Hyde said: "Now as our savior taught us and we are bold to say: 'Our Father who art in heaven . . .'" a light came on in my brain. The one prayer the Bible asserts to have come directly from Jesus does not say: "Jesus' Father who art in heaven"; it says "*Our* Father."

Mating this with the history lesson I'd had the Friday before, it occurred to me that we had mangled the teachings of the one we professed to follow. When Jesus arrived on the scene, monotheism was already established, as was loving thy neighbor and not killing one another. Moses had brought these tenets, carved on tablets of stone, down from the mountain. The revolutionary concept that Jesus gave to the world, the stunning departure from his forebears that was sufficient to get Him killed and to start a new religion, was that we ourselves were a very real part of the divine. Us, you and me and the rotter next door who steals our paper and spends Sunday reading it and swilling beer.

Jesus did not set Himself up as a god, or even as a unique and special relative of God; He did not put himself above others. He taught that each and every human being was a child of God, that the divine was in us, through us, and by us as the children of God. Perhaps this was the message that rocked the world, because it placed the responsibility for good and evil, for godliness and devilry, firmly on our shoulders and made moot the role of priests and rabbis, prophets and seers. If so, it's no wonder that some of the religious leaders of the day saw fit to have Him removed. Their jobs were on the line.

This teaching insisting, as it did, that each and every sweaty, uneducated, heathen bum was equal in God's eyes to the bishop—was onerous, not only to His followers who, in later years, felt the need to deify Him and to place themselves in His place as earthly leaders but to the structure of the Christian church as it began to take on a bureaucratic life of its own.

If one were to follow not the Nicene Creed but the tiny kernel of teachings that are purported to come directly from Jesus of Nazareth, then a heavy burden of both responsibility and joy must be embraced. If, as He said, we are the genuine honest-to-God children of heaven, and we accept the teachings of Jesus to be right and true, then it behooves us to look to ourselves for answers, to know that the miraculous spark that is life and flits momentarily through this pile of muscle and bone is God, the *is*ness of is, the great I Am. We must bear the weight of knowing we are the hands of God that lift others from misery. We are the eyes of God that see each sparrow fall. We are the heart of God that bleeds when His works are defiled and despoiled.

This is indeed a cross to bear. It moves us from prayer to action, forces us to cease putting the evils of the world on the altar for the divine to fix and to get up off our knees and fix it ourselves.

The joy comes in the empowerment and the knowledge that we can move mountains and effect change. And the greatest joy in that we are not alone, abandoned. God is in us and all around us. All we need do to connect is to reach out a hand in love to another living being.

do animals have souls?

Of course they do. Don't be an idiot.

Good, now that we've got *that* settled once and for all, does it ever amaze and delight you to the very core of your being that of all the places in the world, the cool grassy nests under the hedgerows, soft pillows on the daybed, warm patches of sun on a thick carpet, the cat chooses to sit on *your* lap? Me too. When my mind is not too cluttered with nonsense and I take the time—and am coincidentally blessed with a cat's condescension—I marvel at the unparalleled joy and comfort I receive from and give to creatures of another species.

Given humans' covetous and essentially capitalist nature, it strikes me as perfectly normal that we conquered and enslaved animals to do our work and provide us with food. Conquering and enslaving is what Homo sapiens excel at. We have successfully conquered and enslaved each other, rivers, waterfalls, meadows, and even mountains of granite to build our temples. Animals were a pushover.

To use our fellow creatures is natural. To be able to love and be loved by them is incredible. Household pets—and this is a wide category including such varied beasts as tarantulas (which don't count) to horses (which I will grant on anecdotal evidence)—are virtually useless. The less honest among us mutter about dogs for protection and cats to catch mice, but most of that's just fog. My sister's Persian cats would be baffled and alarmed by a genuine rodent, and the dog my mother keeps for "protection" weighs thirteen pounds.

We simply love them. On days when loving other humans is complex and difficult I think the only uncluttered love we are allowed is this odd communion with furry beasts. I believe we are unique in this. I know animals become friends with other animals. Two of my four cats are very fond of their dogs. But we alone seem to be willing to love, shelter, feed, care for, and, oftener than one might think, sacrifice for a member of another species.

I doubt, though I cannot swear never having been put to the test, that, were I starving to death, I would eat Zeb or Mack, Bubba, or Skitzi with any more relish than I would my sister or my husband. In a world where selfless love, true love, dependable love, healthy love can sometimes be at a premium, I believe this love between the animals and humans cannot be overrated.

There are many Christian teachings I might argue with, but the tritest of them all rings true: God is Love.

Just that: the ability to experience love, to feel it, to know it, to share it. That sensation moving through us is the only measurable touch of the godly that most of us will ever get. Taste, touch, hearing, sight, sense of smell are the things of the world that we can experience through the nerves of our body. Love is the thing of heaven that we can only experience through the means of our soul.

My beloved little critters never let me forget this and, because to them I am a kind of god, having power over their lives and deaths and the cupboard where the smoked pigs' ears are kept, they remind me that I am needed; that I am powerful; that I must be kind and I must be responsible or lives could be harmed or even lost. Their trust that I will be all these things keeps me humble.

That they continue to love me when I'm being a jackass keeps me linked to God.

darlin'

Something most peculiar happened to me a while back. I was in Oxford, Mississippi, at Square Books doing a speaking and signing engagement for *Blood Lure.* I'd been signing for maybe fifteen minutes when a young man came up to the table. He was twenty or twenty-two—it crossed my mind to say I was old enough to be his mother, but chances are his mom's a good eight or ten years younger than me. Dark shiny hair fell from a center part to past his shoulders. He was lean, dark-eyed, and probably stoned out of his mind. He wasn't carrying a book.

He leaned on my table, his hair fell forward, and he said: "Darlin', I love the way you . . ."

There was a good deal after that, but I can't remember any of it except that he called me "darlin'" a couple more times. My knees went weak, my head swam, my heart pounded. I had instantaneously reached that state of walking into walls.

Because I am an adult and have had many years training in the art of dissembling, I did not fall out of my chair or begin speaking in tongues. Though I'm sure one or two intuitive women in the crowd noticed my psycho-sexual center had been short-circuited—surely there had been sparks and the smell of burning ozone—I believe the moment of my undoing passed unnoticed.

By great good fortune this disturbance in my universe was fairly short-lived and left behind no addictive cravings for pretty boys with soft hair and stoned eyes. I finished the signing and went home.

So unsettling was the event that I thought about it for several days afterward. It had been a long time since I had been blindsided by a passion like that. As a happily married woman I can't think of anything more frightening than a force of nature such as I'd experienced lasting more than fifteen seconds. Had it lasted days or weeks, I expect I would have been miserable at best and adulterous at worst.

Having lost one marriage and so knowing the preciousness of a husband, a home, a life of decency, friendship, and trust, I wanted very much to figure out *what the hell happened up there.*

I don't have a weakness for younger men. Though I appreciate their natural strength and beauty, I can't imagine they've had the time or experience to develop the warmth, tolerance, and humor that I find thrilling. I love flattery, but I know it's a form of love, not for me, but for my work or my momentary celebrity or my perceived power. And he didn't even buy a book, for chrissake. How flattering is that?

So why the lightning bolt?

For a while I bruited about the idea that what had triggered such a stunning reaction on my part was that this man had stepped right out of my past. He looked like the boys I'd loved in college—David and Duncan and Bruce, Mike and Pat and Steve. Long hair, dressed in Salvation Army chic, eyes full of drug-induced dreams, slow smile, hands not yet cracked or calloused with real work.

In a bookstore in northern Mississippi, my thoughts went, I had merely run, psychically speaking, into a time warp; met a flashback in the flesh.

I rather liked that explanation. It fit a lot of familiar comfortable theories of post-traumatic stress syndrome and early childhood trauma. I sat with it for a bit, but in the end, fond of it as I'd grown, I had to abandon it. I've met dozens of lovely, long-haired men and boys in recent years. A few of them were even stoned. I enjoyed them but suffered no disruptions to the wiring of my brain. It wasn't the way the young man in Oxford looked, or moved, or the sweet smell of dope smoke and cologne emanating from his clothes.

He'd called me darlin'.

No kidding, that was it. No man had ever called me darlin' before. How was I to know the staggering effect it would have? I don't think the boy intended to raze my emotional walls. Here in the South, terms of endearment are tossed around with impunity. Honey, Sweetie, and Sugar take the place of the Yankee's Buddy and Hey You.

At first, realizing a word had unwomanned me, I couldn't help but think, *How shallow can you get? A boy calls you darlin' and you're ready to give him your phone number, credit cards, and your husband's first-born son.*

This self-castigation didn't last. I'm forty-nine years old. Forty-eight of those have been spent in self-examination. I'm just not that shallow.

". . . raze my emotional walls." That thought floated back, and I realized that I did have emotional walls, walls between the world—even the small part of the world which genuinely loves me—and my innermost vulnerable woman's heart; the fragile part of me that believes in true love, soulmates, and Cary Grant.

Maybe it's Cary Grant's fault (though I know Cary Grant would never drop his g's) that "darlin' " spoken with warm intent was the key that opened a door so long locked and so obscured by baggage I didn't even know it was there. The romance of movies, books, the belief in love at first sight and Happily Ever After were synthesized in one word, a word that went out of fashion when the elegant actors and optimistic writers of the thirties and forties faded from public view. Perhaps it had come to symbolize the part of me that had once believed I would be taken care of and all that would be asked in return would be love.

This wee forgotten corner of myself was where I'd never been hurt, never hurt another. I could respond with a completeness that swept away decades of cynicism and betrayals both petty and profound.

It pleases me that innocence still exists in some corner of my soul and saddens me that the corner had to be shut away to keep it safe. This must be the place in all of us where we love with absolute abandon and confidence. That freedom was what overwhelmed me, an outpouring so unguarded it frightened and unsettled me. The knowledge it exists reassures me that a primal and powerful ability to love without fear is part of our human makeup.

Because of the sexual overtones of this sudden tsunami of feeling, I hesitate to use the terms "love" and "innocence"—those things we associate with little girls in white Communion dresses, lambs, and whiskers on kittens—and this was most assuredly not a fragile, delicate or, very possibly, ladylike sensation. But it was womanly. If innocence can be defined as passionate trust, as innocence of pain or betrayal, then I was afforded a glimpse of my psyche that was completely, innocently female.

I don't know if I will ever get back to that forgotten corner. Still, it's good to know that part of me has not been destroyed, merely buried, and the next time a sweet-voiced man looks at me with eyes slightly out of focus and calls me darlin' I may again find my way back to the place where my heart is still new.

faith

Last night I saw a TV commercial advertising furniture and God. The ad was posing as a public service announcement, but the name of the store was featured prominently at the end. Quite tasteless, but it got me to thinking not only about furniture but about our need for the Lord, so perhaps it was not wasted air space. The message was simple: "Everybody needs the Lord." The images were of downtrodden miserable types clearly in need of something.

As I watched, I knew, having been around the block a time or two, that the god of most of our imaginings, the one with whom we plead for intercession, cessation of pain, and whatever else we deem necessary to our lives, is not going to pull our feet from the fire anytime soon. We live in a world where wars are commonplace. Every night on the news we see refugees, starving children, images of destruction and terror, people living horrible lives and dying horrible deaths and, but for the lucky few we read about in the ancient texts, none are rescued by the Lord.

Though many profess to, nobody really knows what God is. Each religion creates an image of God and lays out a series of rules purported to get you on His good side, but the images and rules differ from culture to culture. Given this, it occurred to me that what we need to get through our days is not God but faith.

My sister and I, both prone to the occasional bout of depression, were discussing ways of handling it. Why, we wondered over the phone lines between Mississippi and California, couldn't we just relax, watch a little television, and wait for it to pass the way we would with a headache? The difference was faith. Healthy people, when sick or injured, have faith that they will one day be well. It's faith that keeps their courage up, allows them to endure with patience and a degree of good cheer. Depression, by its very nature, robs one of faith. A major symptom of depression is the feeling it is forever.

I think this holds true for life in general. Those who have faith that life is good, that things will turn out for the best, that suffering is a necessary learning process, faith in *anything,* survive the torments of life better than those who have given up.

Faith masquerades as courage, patience, kindness under stress, generosity, optimism—the things that can make or break a life. If this faith is misplaced—faith in one's own strength, in the abilities of others—there will come a time when it must be repudiated by human limitations. Faith betrayed is a bitterness so deep it scars.

Alcoholics Anonymous suggests merely that one have faith in a "Power greater than ourselves." By putting our faith outside the human arena, we put ourselves in the way of God, a place where we must believe without seeing, trust without contracts, suffer without vengeance. In choosing faith in something over which we have no control, little knowledge, something we cannot taste, touch, or smell, we place that magical part of ourselves that is wholly good beyond the reach of everyday evils. Regardless of what happens to us, we have a place to go where we can rest in the surety that everything will turn out for the best, if not here then somewhere else: heaven, the next life, in joining the flow of the Tao. This faith, this safe place of the soul, allows us to meet life with courage, generosity, and optimism.

And how to find this faith? As the Bard said, "Ah, there's the rub." Some people are born with it, some taught it. For the rest of us, it can be a struggle, and one we may or may not win. The tools we've chosen to build our society do not lend themselves to the task of building or finding faith. Intellect works against us, as does logic, observation, and history. The remaining arrow in our quiver is instinct, and I believe it flies true. Most of us instinctively believe in a Power greater than ourselves. Even atheists have to make a mental note not to pray. When the chips are down, instinct tells us to cry out to *something.* For me, this was enough to begin the germination of faith.

Because I've been saddled with intellect and cynicism, faith was hard for me. I began with the instinct, then chose consciously to pretend to believe simply because it was much too lonely not to. With practice, my faith slowly became real, the playacting moved into the realm of belief. Now it bolsters and comforts me, allows me to be better than I was, stronger, happier.

As a young agnostic/atheist wannabe, I took great pleasure in dismantling others' religious beliefs with the scalpels of logic and ridicule. Now, when someone tries to attack my faith with those same weapons, all I can do is laugh and remember the words of Sister Mary Vionney: "Faith is just that, Nevada. You just *believe.*" It's a sense out of this world; it cannot be touched by words.

It just is.

Or it isn't.

flip-flops, girlfriends, and levi jackets

Three things never fail a girl: old Levi jackets, flip-flops, and girlfriends. Armed with these, any situation can be weathered, if not with grace and aplomb, at least with a modicum of comfort and hope for the future.

Flip-flops are comfortable, pack well, and come in all colors. Like the rattle of a diamondback, they warn people of your approach. Levi jackets are imbued with a soul of cast iron; they never wear out. The older they get, the better they are. A weathered Levi jacket adds a touch of devil-may-care humor and solid practicality to anything from a swimsuit to a prom dress.

Girlfriends I discovered rather late in life. The reason it took me so long was the Myth.

Our society, like a thousand others, is pervaded by myths, things so woven into the cultural mind-set we no longer know how they began, subcutaneous "truths" that get under our skin from the minute we're born and by which we live as we grow.

One of these myths is so obviously untrue its enduring nature amazes me. The Myth that the only good friends, I mean *really* good friends—the kind you can trust utterly and depend upon in a crunch—are men. Buddy movies, coming-of-age stories, and pals-till-the-end war movies have touted the unbreakable bonds between men. Women, on the other hand, are portrayed as petty: they squabble, stab one another in the back, and will abandon one another at the drop of a man.

What a crock.

In my idiosyncratic and totally unscientific research into the matter, I have discovered women are the arbiters, protectors, creators, and healers of friendship. If there were a god of friendship, she would be a goddess.

Women create friendship opportunities for their children, suggest dinner parties to get to know their husband's friends, make sure the kids stay connected to grandparents, aunts, and uncles. It's women who remember birthdays, weddings, bat mitzvahs and First Communions. They inspire, create, and maintain the friendships for the entire family.

But, most gloriously, they are friends with other women.

I speak of this with such fervor because I was a child of the Myth. I am the black-sheep daughter of a black-sheep daughter. In 1944, painfully shy but frighteningly determined, Mom went into the male world of flying and became a professional pilot. Several years thereafter she married Dad, a divorcé eighteen years her senior. Dad was a pilot. Before that he'd been a mule packer in the Idaho Primitive. He adored my sister and me and worshiped the sky Mom flew through. But not because we were women. No indeed. Because, as he often told us, we were not like other women. You know, those vain silly creatures who chatter tediously about dishes and diapers: Women of the Myth.

Needless to say, I spent much of my youth clinging to the tenuous amnesty from femaleness that my father so generously granted the women of his household—as did my mother and sister. I learned to drive tractors and shoot. I wore Levis and boots. I scorned women. I prided myself on being "one of the boys." I boasted that I liked men better than women, that my best friends were men. At parties I fled the "coffee klatch" in the kitchen to join the fascinating world of men around the bar-b-que.

What saved me from this pale and desperate charade, oddly enough, was golf. When I entered my thirties, the men in my circle became infected with the game. After one too many bogies and birdies, I began slipping away to the women's side of the room.

A new world opened up. Women were nothing like I'd been led to believe. They were honest and funny and interesting.

Topics of conversation were not only more varied than those I'd grown accustomed to but went deeper. We laughed more. A lot more.

I began making women friends. My mother, suffering under the triple curse of shyness, men's work, and the Myth as ratified by my father, had no women friends as I was growing up so I had no hint of what to expect. My new friendships grew and deepened and went right on growing and deepening. I discovered women call each other on the phone for no reason, meet for coffee, lunch, movies. They shop together just for the hell of it, visit each other's houses simply to have company while cleaning the attic. In troubled times, women rally around, support, take up the slack. Women share. Everything. It's what they're programmed to do. Maybe it's evolution: while men were out hunting the mastodon and thinking of the dance they'd do around the fire that night to boast of the heroic encounter, women were in the cave, and it's damn sure they were talking. If either gender can be credited with the creation of language, it has to be women. Women talk.

A marvelously insightful fellow whose name I don't recall (if you know who you are, please write so I can give credit where credit is due) said something to this effect: "Men talk about three things: money, sports, and sex. They exaggerate how much money they make, pretend to know more about sports than they do, and lie about sex. Women talk about only one thing: sex. And they *never* lie . . ."

Occasionally we do talk of other things besides sex, but we seldom lie. Oh, we lie to our bosses, our mothers, our husbands, sons, children, loan officers but not to each other. To lie to a girlfriend is simply missing the point.

Girlfriends don't love you because you are good or rich or beautiful. They love you because you're you, because you love them. They love you because, in the face of adversity, you hurl yourself facedown, cry and wail: "I can't go on." Then you get up and go on. They love you because you go to church on Sunday like you ought to. They love you because instead of going to church on Sunday like you ought to, you stay home and stencil leaves on the bathroom ceiling.

When you love *him,* they love *him;* when you hate *him,* they hate *him.* When you love *him* again, they kindly forget you ever said all those awful things. Not because they think you are right, but because they understand.

During the time I was destroying my first marriage, one of my oldest friends, Debbie, was very angry. Not at me for committing adultery. Oh no. At my husband for lying about *how many times.* Now that's a girlfriend.

Having come into this place of women later in life, I not only notice and celebrate these ties but marvel that this deep, rich, funny, connected society has bubbled along under the surface mostly unnoticed by men and largely unremarked upon. The only thing I can attribute this to is that, till recently, most books published, movies made, and television shows produced were conceived of, written by, and starred men. They didn't know—or possibly didn't care to know—about the bonds between women, and so created, then perpetuated, the Myth of male friendships and female isolation.

A friend of mine, who is the most brilliant and sensitive of men, joined the men's group my husband belongs to a while back. After several meetings, he was delighted with the support and camaraderie. So, one Tuesday morning, a morning we met to talk of writing, God, hats, evil, and the like, he says to me: "You know, I think men may be ahead of women in this. A next step in spiritual evolution. Men are getting together, forming groups, *talking.* Maybe women should do that."

Do that? We live that. Getting together to talk and support one another and talk and problem-solve and talk is so old a tradition among women that no one even takes note of it. It's like air or water, life-sustaining things we take for granted until for one reason or another service is interrupted. And, unlike men's groups, though I am speaking from an outsider's point of view and things may have changed, women don't put limitations on what they can talk about, what they can confess to, what will be forgiven or understood.

Women are born into a support group. All we need do, it seems, is embrace it.

Girlfriends are warmer than Levi jackets, stronger, and can take you to as many places. The older they get, the more comfortable they are. They keep you warm, keep you fashionable, keep you from being too vain while letting you be as silly as you need to be. Like flip-flops, they can walk through mud with you and emerge undamaged, make you laugh when all else fails, and keep you from taking yourself too seriously.

Maybe women developed these complex and life-affirming ties to better care for our children. Perhaps it evolved because it was the best way to get the work done that needed doing. Maybe we clung together to survive emotionally in a male-dominated world. It might be an evolutionary trait to better the chance of offspring surviving.

Or, could be, it's a gift from God because she likes us best.

salvation

"For us and for our salvation, He came down from heaven."

But salvation from what? The easy answer is death. Since none of us know anybody who was permanently saved from death, and anything that happens after that is pure speculation—or faith, if you like—maybe there is a more practical application of the concept of earthly salvation. Maybe the teachings of the prophets were given to us to save us from never having lived, from the little deaths that creep in and rob us of joy and strength and, in the end, cause us to pass our time here in a nightmare, asleep at the wheel, frittering away our precious moments of life.

My mother, who turns seventy-eight this year and is blessed with good health and a wonderful mind, was telling me she is aware now like she's never been before that life is precious, every moment of it. When she finds herself muttering along, mind full of pesky details and frets, she wakes herself up by saying: "By God, where is the JOY?" She then takes the time to look around her and see it, appreciate it, experience it. There is such joy to be found in her snug little house, her Jack Russell terrier, her cats, her hot tub and, it is to be hoped, her two daughters.

Being from good stock, Mom's probably got another twenty years or so of joy to look forward to.

Most of us in America are among the fortunate. We are not starving, we are not in unbearable pain. Given these burdens, finding the kernel of *life* in our life, though I believe it can be done, would be a lot trickier. For the rest of us there is abundant joy if we are *saved*. Much to my immense surprise and no little embarrassment, it took Jesus of Nazareth and the teachings left by His followers to lead me to this promised land. There are many ways to get there, I'm sure, but this was mine. When I joined the church, I never expected to be "saved." I was painfully aware I needed saving, but from what I wasn't sure. From despair, I expect.

In following the words, because I had nothing better to do and no other pathways happened to be open to me at that time, I learned to share, to be in community, to have faith—if not in the god of the Episcopal church, at least in some of its people, some of the time. I learned to have faith in myself. I learned gratitude, forgiveness, sacrifice, turning the other cheek—those annoying things much touted by grandmothers and nuns.

And I'll be damned if I wasn't eventually saved. Saved in the sense that I began to live my life instead of scripting it, trying to manipulate it, rewrite it, drown it, sleep through it, or abandon it altogether by attempting to live someone else's life for them or a life of fantasy that needn't take me out of my easy chair.

Moses, via the tablets and the mountain, brought us warnings of what to avoid if we wished to be saved: envy, greed, adultery, idolatry, murder, theft, denigrating others, denying honor to those who should be honored. When we embrace these things, we bite off a wee bit of death, chew it up, and swallow it. In greed and envy we lose the joy in the things that are ours. Adultery is the end of trust and love and self-respect. Instead of knowing love and trust, we know only guilt, hardship, anger. Stealing and murder fill our souls with plots, fears, paranoias. Instead of knowing friendship and safety, we dwell in a shadow world where nothing is as it seems. In not honoring the people in our lives who deserve to be honored, we lose the concept of respect and admiration both for others and for ourselves. It is the death of heroes and hope, of finding those whom we deem honorable and so learning how to become honorable ourselves. Months or years slip past as if we were the walking dead, rambling through hell.

Even when our lives are at their most fractured, our days pushed through a tangle of fears so thick that we can scarcely draw breath, most of us know with some tiny part of our hearts that there is something else.

Those who have never known peace or plenty sense that there is a world where peace and plenty abound. Over the centuries cultures have named this place: Valhalla, Nirvana, Heaven. We have sung of it, painted its landscapes, dreamed its angels. Often it is the only thing that keeps us from despair, keeps us putting one foot in front of the other.

In this country, we know plenty and freedom from fear. We do not know peace, but we sense its existence. We sense how rich and real and *lively* our lives would be if we could attain it.

Salvation brings this peace. The prophets and seers and saints teach us how to be alive, how to avoid the destroyers of color, light, and freedom. When we choose to be "saved," to honor the teachers that have been given us, lessons that have proved worthy over the years, in place of living death we are given a real live life, for however many years we are allotted on this earth.

If it so happens there is life after death in one form or another, that is all to the good. Till then, I believe in embracing this life, the one that He came down to heaven to save for me.

an ordinary life

When I was young I thought only the big things, dramatic, impressive things, could make me truly happy. I lusted after romance on a grand scale: Rhett and Scarlet, Romeo and Juliet, Tristan and Isolde. I wanted to live like Errol Flynn, and when I died, I wanted to die like Camille.

Edna St. Vincent Millay had already written my epitaph:

My candle burns at both ends;
It will not last the night;
But, ah my foes, and, oh, my friends—
It gives a lovely light.

Anything less, I thought, was "settling," giving up, a life of quiet desperation. I pitied the normal, scorned the average, and snubbed the straight and narrow. Had someone told me then that "may you live in interesting times" was a curse and not the stuff of New Year's good wishes I would have been baffled.

After a time—a very long time, as this view of life was deeply ingrained—it became clear to me why Hamlet is a young man. Only the young can sustain a high level of intense emotion for any length of time without crumpling under the strain. And only the young are sufficiently naïve as to see pain as anything but pain and glamour as anything but a fabrication.

Even as I write this I feel a mild compulsion to explain, to make it clear that eschewing the black-and-white ideals of True Love, soulmates, heroic sacrifice, the imagined glamour of tragedy, pain, and death is not to live a half-life in a world comprised of shades of gray; that "ordinary" isn't a bad word.

In fact, I've come to love the ordinary. A life ago, I was depressed, broke, homeless, unemployed, and divorced. While wandering dispiritedly around a general store in Durango, Colorado, I saw a pretty tin, Italian-looking, designed for storing spaghetti. Quite without self-pity, merely as a statement of fact, I thought, "If I were an ordinary person, I could have a tin like that." At the time a spaghetti tin with its connotations of a kitchen to keep it in, a stove to cook the pasta on, and a husband to share it with were fantastic dreams.

But now I have managed, at long last, an ordinary life. In the ordinary, I have discovered that the very things I once scoffed at are the greatest gifts.

High drama is the stuff of the stage: artificial, man-made. The ordinary is from God. Oh, once in a while, the heavens give in to a spate of drama: earthquakes, hurricanes, floods. But mostly it's us, us with our schemes and wars and broken hearts, who provide the theatrics.

The ordinary I found ready-made. A kitten, a cup of tea, a lily, a weeping willow, a good night's sleep, a letter from a friend: these everyday things began to unfold before me in a breathtaking way.

Anybody can get a kitten. Kittens are so common the pound routinely kills hundreds because they are too numerous. Yet here is a perfect creature, warm, furry, fun, and funny—a live *animal* you can hold, listen to it purr, watch it chase leaves. You can have this incomprehensible miracle in your house, in your *lap,* for heaven's sake.

And tea! A magnificent beverage from China or England or Thailand, grown in fields by people who live on the other side of the world, brought into your very own home for your enjoyment. Amazing.

Lilies, willows—the fabric of fairy tales. Flowers of myriad shapes, hues, and scents, plants higher than a house, strong enough to climb in, and you can actually *grow* these things. Right in your own backyard. Incredible.

Even True Love, I mean truly true love, is ordinary. No crawling across the burning sands, just doing up the dishes; not slaying dragons but holding hands at the movies, letting you have the last Oreo, bringing you a medicinal cat when you're sick in bed. The stuff of dreams.

A couple of years ago, I saw that spaghetti tin, this time in a local department store. I bought it. Now it sits on the counter in my suburban kitchen, filled with supermarket spaghetti. Last night my husband boiled some up, poured store-bought sauce over it, and brought me a bowl where I sat on my couch in my Sears polyester pajamas. Nothing out of the ordinary—just your standard, mundane, run-of-the-mill miracle.

I was extraordinarily happy.

pain

Somewhere along the line I got the impression pain was currency. Maybe it just leaked into my subconscious by way of the Judeo-Christian ethic—mostly the Christian—that to suffer was a good thing, could earn one a place in heaven. Or it could be that I was just spoiled rotten by my father. At any rate, I came into adulthood thinking that if I suffered enough, I could somehow get my own way; that pain could be exchanged for forgiveness, acceptance, success, or strength.

This cognitive distortion is not limited to me alone. A friend of mine, who has suffered from depression since her husband died, only just recently chose to go on medication for it. Even now, feeling so much better and beginning to get her life back on track, she is quick to say the depression medication she is on is different from the others, mild, hardly anything at all. Why? Because she is a strong woman. She doesn't run to the doctor. She handles her own problems. I've heard people brag (and, indeed, have probably been one of these braggarts) that they got over pain—either emotional of physical—without the crutch of drugs, up by the old bootstraps, as it were. The implication was clear: those of us who did use something to kill the pain were weaker, less deserving, had failed, caved in in some manner.

We have been taught pain makes us strong. To endure is good. In adherence to this ingrained misinformation, a lot of us have allowed ourselves to become addicted to emotional, if not physical, pain. I remember an unfortunate woman I knew in Minnesota. In unkind moments, her friends would joke that when she introduced herself, she'd say: "Hi, my name is Alison and *I'm in pain.*" There was some truth to the joke. She had come to hold pain as an important aspect of her personality; suffering as a replacement for real relationship to others or self. Another woman of my acquaintance converted her pain into anger and used it to indicate she was not one of the common folk willing to turn a blind eye to the evils of the world, that, unlike us tawdry happy people, she was too good to settle for less.

I've never quite succumbed to this level of pain addiction, but I have come close. There've been times I clung to my pain in the belief it would earn me a place in whatever heaven I was coveting at the moment. I have also held pain close to my heart in the mistaken belief that to let go of it would let someone else off the hook, as if my pain, held and nurtured, would magically transfer to the person who had hurt me.

A few years back I decided I simply must get off antidepressants. Taking them shamed me and made me feel weak. I quit taking the drug and, over the next five weeks, proceeded to spiral down into the dark places. I was in church one evening and I was praying loudly (in mind, not in mouth): "Dear God, what shall I do? Help me? What can I do?" A voice in my head yelled back: "Take the damn medicine." Following that unambiguous communiqué, my view of pain changed. I came to the conclusion that pain is nothing but pain, a cry from the body or the soul to be healed.

Pain itself is merely an alarm bell set off to indicate all is not well, but, in and of itself, it has no value. It is not the coin of the realm or an indicator of personal worth. When suffering intense pain, the clanging of nerves takes up so much focus and energy neither the body nor the mind can do the work needed. I know when I am in pain it's hard to be kind, generous, understanding, productive, giving. It's all I can do just to keep my own head above water. Pain does not make me a better person; it makes me petty and crabby and selfish. And it makes me a liability to others.

In law enforcement and emergency rescue one of the things drummed into your head in training is Officer Safety. If an emergency medical technician or a policeman or park ranger comes on the scene to rescue someone and allows themselves to be injured either by carelessness or irresponsible heroics, the rescuer then becomes another victim who must be dealt with.

The same holds true in daily life. If we allow ourselves to be drawn into the pain of others, to become overtired or embittered in serving our fellows, we become of no use to anyone and a burden to many. The martyr only believes herself to be suffering for others. Mostly her suffering is harming others whether she intended it to or not.

I have come to believe that it is a duty to relieve our own pain. It is a responsibility to stay fit and healthy to live long and well for our children and friends. When we hurt, it is a duty to relieve that pain so we do not inflict it on others, so we do not lose our kindness and productivity.

The medical community has found ways to relieve much physical pain. Slowly, we've come to accept that it is not a sign of inferiority to take an analgesic when we hurt. Drugs for emotional pain have not yet received that acceptance, but it's time they did. Time we abandoned the concept that suffering is *good.*

This idea brings to mind a soft, whiny society of overgrown infants, but because we are fragile and because life can be hard, I believe there will still be enough pain around to keep us on our toes and teach us our daily lessons.

taking shit

Several years after I went into law enforcement in 1989, I was at my annual forty-hour refresher course for park rangers in Apostle Islands National Lake Shore. We had a crusty old Wisconsin sheriff as a guest speaker for one of the classes. First he asked the group what they did when citizens of an unsavory stripe talked back. One young man (from which park, I don't remember), a studly fellow broad in the shoulders and short in the neck, said: "I don't take shit off anybody. They give me shit, I take action."

I was shrinking down into my seat wondering if this scatological reference to the hostilities sometimes heaped upon the uniform was the right answer and wishing I was a macho dude and not so small and female and verbal.

The sheriff looked at this strong, outspoken young ranger and said: "As a law-enforcement officer it's your *job* to take shit. Punks smart mouth you, you take it. Drunks vomit on you, you take it. Ladies spit at you because you wrote 'em a ticket, you take it. Taking shit is what we do. You damn well better get good at it."

I found tremendous wisdom in this. Once the concept that I was too good or too strong or too important to "take shit" from anybody had been stripped away from me, once I had been not only given permission but told it was my sworn duty to "take shit," the work I'd chosen took on a different cast. What the sheriff had done was to factor pride and ego out of the mix. I no longer had to defend my image — whatever that was—but could focus on handling any situation that came into my purview: calm those who needed calming, educate those who needed educating, arrest those who needed arresting. To continue with the earthy metaphors, I no longer had to enter into pissing contests that served only to expend energy, waste time, and escalate the situation to the next level of violence.

While speaking with my sister on the telephone, we lamented how much we hated being "messed with." Having people come into our neat little worlds and fiddle around, mucking things up, thwarting our plans, and ruining our schedules. And everybody messes with you: doctors mess with you, the electric company, the IRS, the kids next door, sisters and cousins and aunts mess with you.

After we hung up, having had a fine wallow, it crossed my mind that what holds true for men and women in uniform holds true for the rest of us.

Should we choose to stay in society, in relationship to other people, rather than sit meditatively in a cave on a mountaintop, then perhaps it is our *job* to be messed with. Not that I advocate being taken advantage of or, God forbid, abused—it is my hope that everyone reading this has a pretty good idea of the difference.

In a country as rich and technologically advanced as America, being messed with happens more and more. We are not the rugged individualists on the prairie, churning our own butter, harvesting our own wheat, and grinding it to bake our own bread. We live in matrix with the hundreds of thousands of others who provide goods and services and to whom we, in turn, provide goods and services. My country-dwelling mother laughs at me because not only do I not know where my water comes from, I don't much care. I only care that it is there when I turn on the faucet.

Since "messed with" is not in the *OED,* I'd better define my terms. In my mind the term means to have others infringe, impinge, thwart, irritate, annoy, aggravate, discombobulate, and inconvenience Me while seeking pursuits of their own. This would include but is not limited to slow clerks, surly waiters, rude cell phone owners, bad drivers, ignorant public servants, lazy contractors—in other words, all the people out there who don't let me do what I want when I want to for legitimate but (in my eyes) ridiculous reasons of their own.

There have been times I've responded to these stumbling blocks to my personal peace as if I had been insulted. My pride whispers, "How dare they mess with Me. How dare they suggest I do not know what is best. How dare they think I would be evil, stupid, lazy."

When I can shift perspective to that of the sheriff and focus not on the self-righteous anger but on the task at hand, I find not only do I save myself a good deal of angst, but I am far more likely to get what I want. When I can look upon accepting these annoyances, keeping business on an even keel and spreading as little mayhem and heartburn as possible as my *job* as a member of this social group, dealing with them becomes almost easy.

The other payoff in doing this is that when I fail and, as people here in Mississippi are wont to say, show my butt, instead of feeling I am a monster, I can think: "Well, I failed to do my job. Next time I will do better."

We used to have a framework for handling situations where we deemed we were being messed with. It was called good manners. Good manners have fallen by the wayside as we've become richer, busier, more frazzled, and more self-important. Maybe if we look upon good manners not as an option but as our job as members of a tribe, it won't seem quite so difficult.

Anyway, that's going to be my plan. Wish me luck.

service

During the decade-long winter of my discontent I had the opportunity to visit a great number of psychologists, psychiatrists, and family counselors. There were as many diagnoses as to what my "problem" was and what should be done about it as there were practitioners of the art of mental healing.

They disagreed on diet, drugs, talk therapies, art therapies, hypnosis, regression—you name it. From this confusing and contradictory cacophony only two treatments for depression were universally agreed upon.

The first was exercise. Everybody told me physical exercise was a good weapon in the fight against the creeping midnight of the soul. This made sense: increased circulation, oxygen to the brain and all that. Some spoke of "endorphins" but, like runner's high, the Holy Grail, and multiple orgasms, I had to take that on faith. But I can attest to an immediate and dependable benefit of exercise. After a trip to the gym I enjoy a glow of smug self-righteousness that can last an hour or more. During bleak times, that hour was often the only good time and therefore cannot be undervalued.

The second prescription against misery that the professionals agreed on was service. When one suffers from depression, it lifts the spirits to be of service to another person. Every one of them told me this.

When I asked why, I received fairly standard answers: it takes your mind off yourself, it shows you other people are as bad or worse off than you, it gives you a sense of control, self-worth.

Those things are valid as far as they go. Being a culture which has pretty much thrown over the traces of religion and faith for science and psychiatry, we tend to want things explained in ways that we can understand. We want things to be logical, clinical. Self-interest is an extremely logical way to look at service. Evolution is based on luck and self-interest.

I still exercise regularly to enjoy smug self-righteousness, but I believe service to others has a value that manifests in a much deeper way than mere self-interest. I've come home to that old aphorism: Virtue is its own reward.

I think helping others makes us feel good not because it's a distraction but because it's THE RIGHT THING TO DO. I have also come to believe there is cosmic right and wrong that transcends logic and that doing the right thing, though often expensive and inconvenient, usually makes us feel good. Like working hard, sleeping soundly, hearing birds sing or kittens purr, being *good* is what we were designed to do and, when we do it, it feels right.

How do I know what's right? Sometimes I don't. But mostly I do. So do you. I suppose this knowledge comes to each of us in a different way. For me, it's sort of like a low-wattage refrigerator light on a bad electrical circuit. When I am mentally opening doors, looking at actions I might take in any given situation, when I happen to snatch open the door on the action that is *right,* a weak light flickers in the back of my mind. I've no interest in whether it's nature or nurture, God or Mom, I only care that it's there. Knowing the right thing usually happens early on, but too often, self-interest butts in with a fog of logic and my little light is obscured.

When I've consistently ignored this little light, I've run the risk of losing it altogether. I don't think our sensors for right abandon us, but it seems we can train ourselves not to notice them. Like agility, strength, and intelligence, the sense of right must be exercised to keep it strong.

There are no spiritual sciences, just anecdotal tales handed down by word of mouth. I am not a proponent of trying to codify the spiritual, isolate its essence, and inject it into lab rats to see if it makes them happier. But there are spiritual laws that can be sensed if I am quiet and open.

I have wandered many paths. I have been a jerk. But I've also been a pretty decent human being. And I know that when I align myself with natural tendencies toward good, when I help someone or stop a bad act, or tend to an abandoned creature not for any personal gain but because it is the RIGHT THING TO DO, life is better.

seeing

As I mentioned, my mother is in her late seventies. Because of clean living, good luck, and good genes, she's strong and active. She hikes, snorkels, kayaks, shovels snow; her back is straight, her stride is long and sure. Each autumn she goes to the island of St. John for a week in a time-share condo. This October she called to say she'd arrived safe and sound but was a bit shocked by a series of incidents which had transpired on the four legs of her air journey.

She told me: "Not once, not twice, but *three* times some nice young person at an airport asked me if I needed a wheelchair. They saw me as a little old lady. . . . I guess I *am* a little old lady."

A woman who goes to church with me, a lady blessed with naturally curly (and once red) hair so forgiving it would look adorable if the dog gnawed on it, is in the habit of cutting her own hair. Several months ago, just to see how the other half lives, she decided to get a salon cut. She was sitting in the half-trance beauty parlors induce when she noticed the floor was covered with snow-white hair. She told me: "I thought, 'Oh for heaven's sake! Don't they even bother to sweep up between customers?' Then I realized all that white hair was mine."

Recently I was in Asheville, North Carolina, with a couple of girlfriends to enjoy the Biltmore Estate and the fall colors. I asked Betty, the eldest of our group at seventy-seven, if she'd started to feel old yet. She said: "No. Other than the aches and pains, I still feel like me."

There is, it would seem, some sort of essential "me-ness."

I don't know that this "me" is ageless, changeless, or infinite. I know that in many fundamental ways my behavior, my outlook, even my thoughts have changed. As slings and arrows have hit home, I've morphed into a more compassionate woman. But I can't say for sure whether the essential me-ness has been altered in any way or whether I've merely been forced to learn a better way to get along with others.

On a gut level, I feel that that bit of me-ness—that soul, if you will—has remained unchanged; that it was pure and perfect to begin with and has remained pure and perfect despite the rigors of life. I am at the mid-century mark and have not yet suffered having Boy Scouts offer to help me across the street but, true to genetics, my hair is rapidly going white, and it won't be long before these lads begin to look at me with merit badges dancing before their eyes. I am with Jack Benny; in mind at least, I am eternally thirty-nine. I suffer a mild schism when what the outside world perceives no longer jives with this image—an image that sticks for Lord knows what reason—that I have decided expresses my inside, and they see old or stuffy or female instead of *me.* The true me. The unchanging me.

What a peculiar happenstance.

Despite all the can't-judge-a-book-by-its-cover lessons I've been taught, I fall into this habit myself. When I see an old tottery person, I see an OLD person, not an old PERSON, if you get my drift.

This rift between body and self speaks of a basic devaluation of the *me*—the soul. Capitalism, crass commercialism, or just the robust youth of our country have caused us to put the value on the packaging and not the gift inside. When the package begins to look weathered, corners bent and ribbons untied, most of us lose interest in opening the gift at all. This may explain our love affair with plastic surgery, hair plugs, dye, and makeup. We know we still exist and we are still *us,* so when the world ceases to see us, value us, we strive to regain the outward form that once made us visible.

We admire strength, agility, quickness, youth, beauty: things of the material body. We find these attributes so seductive that we condemn people who no longer have them to the ranks of the unseen. We look away from the man in the wheelchair, the obese woman. If we deign to pretend they are of interest, we do so with a sense of doing a good deed.

My girlfriend Mari once told me the shock she felt on realizing other people were as *real* as she was. It reminded me of a children's story, *The Velveteen Rabbit,* which tells of a stuffed bunny given to a baby. Over the years this lovely toy is kissed and hugged and slept on and dragged about till its fur is patchy, one eye is lost, grubby fingers have left marks on its ears, sticky kisses mar the once-perfect whiskers. At the end of the tale, though the bunny is scarred and battered, it is made real through the alchemy of a child's love.

Perhaps as we grow older, our pelts shabby and our eyes dim, we, like the Velveteen Rabbit, become ever more real. Seeing the white hair on the salon floor, disconnection in the eyes of young people, wheelchairs offered, experience discounted as obsolete—watching the material accoutrements we've used to define our souls drop away—we understand more clearly what is real in ourselves and others.

I vow to try to *see* others. To see an old PERSON, a famous PERSON, a quadriplegic PERSON, a rich PERSON, a powerful PERSON, a mentally handicapped PERSON.

And I will hope, regardless of how my outsides change, someone, somewhere, will always be able to see *me.*

church

As I've mentioned before, I was not raised in any church. For reasons of legal record keeping (or so my folks said—I think they were hedging their bets), at six weeks I was baptized Methodist, never to cross that threshold again. My parents not only did not go to church, they were pointedly anti-church. When the subject came up, Dad would say: "Why go into a dark airless building with a bunch of hypocrites on a beautiful Sunday morning when you can be outside in God's country?"

Until I was in my late forties, I never found a good answer to that argument. Since men make churches and men make religions, why would a True Believer choose to abandon what God made to worship in what man made? Logic suggested the only pure communion with the divine was to be had in nature. Where better to find God but in God's country?

Even after I began attending church each Sunday, singing hymns, reciting prayers, and watching the light change through the stained-glass windows, I was acutely aware that these things I was comforted by, inspired by, were the things of man, not of God. Yet I most assuredly felt a sense of the divine in church. I felt it on the bright days of Easter services, the holidays with the scents and decorations of Christmas and cynical modern children, freckles above and sneakers below, dressed as wise men and angels. I felt it during Lent when the altar grew stark and the readings were of betrayal and loss.

The obvious reason would be that the Christian Bible rang with truth for me, or that Christ himself felt close. This was not the case. The Bible continues to baffle me, an idiosyncratic and fragmented history of a people's search for the divine. Jesus, featured as one would expect in readings and sermons, speaks to me only as a prophet and teacher whose life I find worthy of emulation.

I didn't come to the Episcopal church because I believed in the unbroken lineage of bishops or because I believed in the god to whom they were said to have dedicated themselves. I chose the Episcopal church over a temple, mosque, or churches inhabited by Presbyterians, Catholics, or Baptists because it was close to my apartment and, the evening the whim came upon me to turn to God, the front doors were unlocked. I didn't come to worship. I came because I was lonely, frightened, and desperately unhappy. The church seemed as good a place as any not to be alone till my life took a turn for the better. Had the Elks been meeting on the block that night and accidentally left their door ajar, I expect my life would have taken a very different direction.

So I went to church. I hid among the people. I donated to the crafts fair, gave to the rummage sale, met with the women's group the first and third Wednesday of every month. When it came to me I wanted to be confirmed, I went to the priest and asked him if it would be okay, considering I didn't accept Jesus Christ as my personal savior, didn't believe the Bible was divinely inspired, and wasn't entirely sure about the whole God thing.

Fortunately, Father Andrew had been tending his flock long enough to recognize a lost lamb when one came bleating into his office and put no obstacles in my way.

Now, after six years of faithful attendance, I have finally come to know the answer to my father's question: Why go inside with a bunch of hypocrites instead of staying outdoors in God's country?

Because God made we hypocrites, too. Because when Jesus said, "Wherever two or more gather in my name, I am there," He wasn't just whistling Dixie. The mountain is for finding and adoring God in the wilderness. Church is for finding and adoring God in community: with others, through others, because of others, in spite of others. Only by finding this place of human interaction focused around the need for the spiritual was I able to recognize God in other people and so, in myself. Without community, how would I learn to share? Who would I help? How would I learn to accept help? Would I learn to serve others without others to serve? And could I know how if I wasn't taught? To what would I, a human being, belong to if not to a group of human beings?

With the exception of the very strong and the very neurotic, most of us feel a need to belong, to be in community. Community is God rubbing elbows and passing the tuna casserole, a place we can snuggle down with the divine.

There are times when the illogic of our church's charitable activities stirs my dormant cynicism. I'll find myself thinking, *For chrissake, if we donated as many billable hours to this thing as we've spent blabbing about it we'd have already met our goal.* Then I remember. Yes, it's about helping those in need. Yes, it's about trying to make the world oh-so-slightly better. But most importantly, it's about doing it together, in community.

Though I'd never have suspected it when I began this spiritual journey, God is not separate from people. Sure we are hypocrites, liars, boasters, blasphemers, and cheats, but we are God's hypocrites, liars, boasters, blasphemers, and cheats. The spark is in each of us. When we work together for what we sincerely hope is good, worship together in the belief we will touch God, sing together in the hope He hears our praises, the spark is fanned and God becomes as visible in us as He is in new snow or mornings on a mountain lake.

repentance

Repentance is tricky. There's so much room for less exalted motivations to creep in undetected.

Early on in life, thinking I grasped the significance of repentance, I became a master of the art of apology. I could grovel at the raising of an eyebrow. It stood me in good stead. Often all that was wanted or needed to make someone feel okay again was to take the blame, let them be right, and acknowledge that I was wrong.

My emotions were usually genuine: I felt sorrow, guilt, shame, fear of abandonment—a few of the prime motivators for repentance—but something was missing. After the sorrys were said and the tears wiped up, I might have a sense of disaster averted or guilt acknowledged but none of genuine renewal.

And, too often, amends could not be made. As the saying goes, a wheel, once it's broken, cannot be mended. I remember the shock when I first had an apology used as an invitation to beat me up all over again. My being sorry didn't take away their pain, and damned if they were going to do anything to alleviate mine.

What I failed to understand was that repentance isn't so much about my relationship with the injured party as about my relationship with myself and, through mind, body, and soul, with God.

Though I was sorry for the pain I caused, repentant gestures stemming from my sorrow were always directed outward. I wanted to turn back the clock and make things the way they were.

Repenting is not about changing the past. The past is, if not written in stone, certainly beyond our mortal reach. Repentance is about changing the future.

It isn't only the consequences of a bad act that are harmful. A bad act, even if done in a vacuum in deep space, is toxic, a poisonous seed planted making life a little bleaker. Too many bad acts, however repentant one is, and the roots of misery grow into thickets of wasted emotion. Tangled hurts separate us from others, from ourselves and, so, from God.

True repentance is to turn back, turn back and don't do it

again. If you do plant a poison seed, turn back, choose not to nurture it.

Repentance is not so much about apology, amends, or guilt as about changing your life, turning away from people and ways and acts that are unhealthy; turning back to health, love, light: the things we choose our gods to embody.

bits of string

I'm finally starting to understand why those legendary little old ladies collected bits of string, used mason jars, and paper bags. There was a time when such behavior was attributed to having lived through the Depression, a time without plenty of plenty.

My whole life has been lived in a golden age. I've never wanted for food, clothing, or shelter. I have wanted more and better, but there's never been a time when I was afraid the meal I was eating would be my last or, other than by choice or accidental circumstance, that I would be sleeping out in the rain come sundown. I have been blessed to live in a time of such wealth I have probably thrown away more stuff than a lot of people have ever owned. Not because it was broken or useless, but simply because I grew tired of it, got new and better stuff.

For reasons I'm not wholly cognizant of, the waste is beginning to bother me. Not that I've stopped using, spending, and discarding, mind you, but it has begun to weigh on me. I've begun to think the little old ladies with string were not products of the Depression but women who had come, over a lifetime, to feel the preciousness of the goods the world lays at our feet. It's as if my eyes and my fingers have developed a new sensitivity. At times I can feel the intricate history of mundane items: the tree from which the wood was taken to make a pair of cheap disposable chopsticks in a Chinese restaurant, the life of the workers who manned the factory that made them. I smell the diesel of the boat that brought them to our shores and feel the faint traces of electricity from the lights in the warehouse where the boxes were stored prior to shipping.

Flipping through the endless glossy full-color catalogues that choke my mailbox, it crosses my mind how unbelievably lovely the pictures are, how vibrant and clear, that a thousand years ago only pharaohs and kings could afford such beauty. It stuns me that I can purchase a reproduction Michelangelo for five bucks at Wal-Mart and chuck it into the garbage when a Klimt catches my eye.

My husband and I live in a 2,100-square-foot house, just the two of us, and we haven't enough storage space. Books proliferate, they fill the bookcases, are stacked on the bedstands, slide off the kitchen counter. When I visited the Library of Congress, I went to the rare book room and the librarian showed me illustrated manuscripts from the fifteenth and sixteenth centuries. He talked of the labor-intensive and expensive process books went through to get made. Now I can't hold a book without feeling a reverence for the value once placed on them and the importance they have in my life.

This weird connection to the inanimate is making a string collector of me, causing me to be uncomfortable with the tremendous waste in my life and in the culture in which I live. Having been accustomed to wallowing in goods, it took a jolt to get me to focus on what it was that was haunting me. A few weeks back I was staying at a lovely resort in Asheville, North Carolina. Part of the package deal was two dinners at the fine restaurants there. The meals included appetizer, salad, main course, side dish, and dessert. Each of these courses was big enough to make an entire meal. I ate three of my eight jumbo shrimp, a few bites of my Caesar salad, struggled through a bit of my steak and baked potato, and more or less just fiddled fatly with my apple pie and ice cream. Easily three quarters of that wonderful food was consigned to the garbage can. The next night was even worse, because the mere thought of all the food I was to be responsible for had ruined my appetite. Perhaps because of the peculiar sensitivity I've developed concerning the intricate and irreplaceable nature of the things in my world, the experience unsettled me.

This is a true "meditation" piece in the sense that I have absolutely no solution. Not a clue. I know the food I could not swallow can't very well be sent to the starving children in China. The dresses I wear twice, then give to the Salvation Army will still sell if I don't buy them. SUVs and Cadillacs will drink any gas I save by leaving my Honda in the garage and walking or riding my bicycle.

A *tragedy of the commons* situation exists in America. In a nutshell, if the commons are being overgrazed by sheep and one responsible shepherd ceases to take his animals there, his herd will starve and the other shepherds' sheep will still destroy the commons anyway. At least, this is what I tell myself as I continue to watch an avalanche of riches pour through my hands and down the garbage disposal.

I suppose noticing is the first step, becoming aware of the inherent value and complexity of the things we are given. Appreciation of this led to the sadness and discomfort over the waste.

I guess that is where we might start. First we follow the material goods back through the living beings, plants, and stones that worked and sacrificed to create them. Inevitably that must lead us to the god or gods responsible for the spark of life needed to set the whole thing in motion. When enough of us . . . a grass-roots movement . . . maybe federal legislation . . . a national epiphany . . .

Well, anyway, till then, let's save bits of string.

evil

Evil is a household word these days—I guess it has been for a long time. The Christian tradition comes not only with a god but with a devil. To one, all good is ascribed, to the other, all the bad. Though we talk about evil a great deal and hell and going to hell, there seems to be no consensus on what it is. We've hung onto the concept of our traditional God in His heaven, but we seem to have outgrown Lucifer with his horns and pointy tail and pitchfork. One of the problems with personifying our gods is that we must then ascribe evil to them or personify another, hopefully lesser, god to take the brunt of the hate and fear.

Enemies are handy stand-ins for Satan. When the Cold War ended, we lost a really good devil in the Russians; the Nazis have run their course, and drug lords were getting threadbare. I was thinking we were going to have to go begging for a new devil to put in our movies and our minds till the war against terrorism started. Terrorists make most excellent devils. In so many ways they embody all that is evil: cruelty to the helpless and innocent, tyranny, murder, rape, pillage; the very vision of Beelzebub and his legions.

Evil, as a force outside of ourselves which we can fight with guns and knives, is a solace. It makes us brave, it unites us.

With evil outside, we don't have to take responsibility for the evil inside. I like that. It makes me comfortable. But what if evil is not "out there," not an entity or a force, not an idea or thought, what if it is an *action?* Like mowing the lawn or frying a chicken leg? Maybe there is no Satan, no being, no instigator, maybe evil only is when it *is,* when it *becomes* through rotten behavior. That puts the whole kettle of stinky fish right back into our laps.

The fight then becomes far less dramatic and far more demanding of us as individuals, because our rotten behavior, or the rotten behavior of others, is extremely contagious. An eye for an eye, a tooth for a tooth, a bad act for a bad act; one of the hardest things in the world is not to return evil for evil, not to let it spill over onto the meter-reader or the video store clerk. Perhaps with a strong personality behind the bad acts, a Hitler or a Stalin or an Idi Amin, the bad behavior can become epidemic, a stage set where bad acts are required, expected, or where good behavior is so rare and unrewarded that the bad seems to be the only choice we have.

War, the pandemic of evil, is the medium from which we draw our heroes, those who do good in the face of a tidal wave of bad. But it is off the battlefield where heroes go unrecognized and medals are not given where most of us must face evil.

Evil is in the damage our acts cause and that caused by acts of others. It's the contagion of hate, anger, and spitefulness that we spread when we indulge in our bad acts. Maybe we want to infect the lousy driver who's been on our bumper for six miles, but do we want to infect his wife? His four-year-old daughter? His dog? That's the damage we have to think about when we wish to answer evil with evil, hate with hate.

If we choose to put the devil outside ourselves, maybe that's where he lives, in the spoors of hatred we spew out that go on to hurt people we've never known; the slapped child who grows to abuse her own children, the angry clerk who runs over a cat on his way home, the hurt husband who yells at his secretary. If God is Love, as the saying goes, maybe the devil is hate, the very essence of pain, and we can either contain the devil within or with a bad act we can release him to wreak havoc beyond the borders of our own minds.

commitment

I'd been told I had a problem with commitment, but I blew it off, knowing that the problem was not with my ability to commit but with finding somebody worth committing to. Back then I didn't know commitment wasn't a two-way thing, wasn't about another person. I didn't know it was a choice, and I most certainly didn't know — or wasn't willing to accept—that, much of the time, it's a hell of a lot of work.

I suppose I thought commitment was something the world had to earn. When somebody or something proved itself consistently worthy, then I would commit to it body and soul. The truth is, nothing is "worthy" consistently, not another human being, not a task, not a church. And it is when it or they are not worthy that the commitment comes in, those countless moments when I am not thanked, not appreciated, not rewarded and I still go on loving, doing, because I *said* I would. Don Quixote is the poster boy for commitment: tilting at windmills, romancing hookers, making himself a laughingstock, staying true to his path.

To be committed is to choose to be a fool, to go on with what you've sworn yourself to when those around you are clamoring that you're wasting your time. History is full of heroes who bashed on regardless and, in the end, prevailed: invented the steam engine, proved germs existed, that the world was round and not flat.

Those stories give us courage, but the truth is they are the exceptions. Most of us will never get the world's validation for our commitment. There will never be a moment when everybody finally sees that we were right all along. If we look for the reward, we are doomed either to break this contract with ourselves or suffer the bitterness of the unsung hero.

Even the word "hero" doesn't really apply. A hero must do good for others. True commitment does good for the self. It is our pact with ourselves that we will do a thing. When it's broken, we know our own weakness and suffer the knowledge that we are not to be trusted. Not that others will not trust us, but that we cannot trust ourselves: we will not keep our own promises, finish our own chores, strive unceasingly toward our own goals, stay true to our loved ones.

I still have a problem with commitment. I still want a contract guaranteeing my reward before I commit. But as I practice making commitments, then keeping them, I find myself feeling stronger, more in control of my life. I have a sense of being able to control the direction my little ship takes, and I find my vessel much better able to withstand storms. The fewer promises I break, the less anxious I feel.

Commitment is not a contract with the world but with the self. For me this was both a revelation and a horror. People speak of the right hand not knowing what the left is doing, and that was how I lived. I never knew what I'd do to my life next.

I do not like the concept of having to earn my own trust, but each time I do, I move further from that sense of living with a woman who will not keep her promises, and toward the knowledge that I can trust myself.

alternate lives

Time and again I've heard people saying "if only." If only I'd married so and so . . . If only I'd finished college . . . If only I hadn't . . . I've fallen victim to this line of thought myself. I have my regrets, some of them quite sharp. In my mind was a picture of the life I would have had, if only. This alternate life was rosy, full of joy and fulfillment, and devoid of the heartaches and pains I was currently suffering.

One day I was indulging in this process, this mapping out in mind the lives that had been available to me and were no longer, when an itinerant thought floated in: if only Peter Pan had come to my window instead of Wendy's, I could fly. That image stopped the others in their metaphorical tracks and I laughed. I would dearly love to fly like the Darling children, free and high and in my nightgown. In my dreams, I do quite a bit of it. But, as I've grown older, I've come to accept that it is just a fairy tale. A wonderful fairy tale and a wonderful dream but, short of the miraculous, it ain't gonna happen.

It came to me then that the alternate lives I was whining after, this shining parade of Nevadas I saw marching down the avenues of my mind, were no more based in reality than Peter Pan. They were fictions made up by me; there were no alternate life paths.

There was and is only the life I am living right now, today, the one I try to live cleanly and honestly with varying degrees of success. There is no life when I didn't do the things I did. There is no life when I did the things I think I should have. There is no marriage to so-and-so, no graduation from Juilliard. When I mourn these things as if I had, then lost, them or, worse, resent others or myself because they were "taken from me," I am merely writing tales in my head that make me feel bad. I never lost another life. I never had another life taken from me. Those lives do not exist. All that exists, quite literally and banally, is what *exists.* And that includes my life and times.

The fantasy of going back to the fork in the road and rewriting the past is so prevalent in our literature—Scrooge being visited by Christmases past, present, and future—that I know I'm not the only one who envisions the life I could have had, if only.

Being creatures blessed—or cursed—with the knowledge that there is a past and a future, it makes sense we would dream of controlling it.

Though there is no other life, no other past that would land me on sunnier shores, though there is just the one with its failure and flaws, there are myriad futures, an absolutely dazzling array. Freed from the time and spirit waste of mourning an imaginary future spawned by a fictitious past, there is strength and energy to actualize, to turn this one life's dreams into plans and move forward.

Obsessing on spilled milk and locked nursery windows is an act of laziness and cowardice, a way of ducking responsibility for bettering this one and only life. Real life. Our life.

what if

I was sitting in my spot in the second pew the other day, more or less listening to a visiting priest tell us about a worthy cause, when I was struck with a revelation. Here I was sitting in church on a Sunday morning, folks in robes and carrying crosses and whatnot, talking and singing of God, and I thought, "What if all this is actually TRUE?" Not the particular trappings of this saint or whose prophet was best, not even the bigger questions people like to argue about—which god is the God, whose rules are the Rules—but the whole gestalt of the religions we have been universally compelled to find for ourselves. What if they were true?

What if there is a god, a supermind, a higher power? What if there is an afterlife: heaven, hell, purgatory, nirvana, Mount Olympus, hades? What if the Hindus got it right and we are here on earth, cloaked in imperfect flesh, that we might refine that spark? What if the Christians got the part right about being judged at death and consigned to an eternity of just deserts?

What if we've collectively dreamed this stuff for a hundred thousand years because it's the truth?

What if there really is a soul? I'm not talking some mysterious, breath-of-life, spark-of-God thing but a really real thing; a part of us that exists as necessary and central to our lives as our spines? Something we don't see and we don't create that separates the quick from the dead? And this particular part of us, the soul, is the only organ of the body that has the qualities necessary to survive death, that is eternal, or close enough it makes no difference? What if our essential essence, whatever it is and whatever condition it is in when our bodies die, continues on? If your essence is of joy, you go on in joy. If your essence is anger, you go on in anger. If you have no essence, you continue into nothingness. If this is true, a great deal suddenly makes sense. Virtue *is* it's own reward. Crime *doesn't* pay. Lust, anger, greed, envy, hatred are evils in and of themselves because of the effect they have on our souls, our very selves.

I do believe there is an essence that is in the body, but on some level not *of* the body; an essence that leaves the body when the body dies. I've seen it happen and, since modern science with all it's stunning wizardry still can neither create life nor even tell us from whence it comes or where it goes, I will hang on to my sense that this essence, this soul, is ours, lives within us, goes elsewhere when the body dies.

Should you accept the hypothesis that the soul is real, and it's ours, and it survives after the body dies, here's the scary question: what if we can damage our soul by what we do/say/think/be here on earth? Make this part of us to limp into eternity less than strong, less than whole? That makes the little hairs on the back of my neck stand up. To think of spending eternity with my "sins," with the damage I've done to my *self,* is pretty grim.

The upside would be that, if we can harm our essences, our souls, our selves, then we can refrain from harm and, if we're lucky, we can actually do good, strengthen and refine our selves.

Seeing the immortal soul not as a sort of get-out-of-jail free card where you list your good deeds and, if they are sufficient, St. Peter opens the pearly gates, but as something living, something that continues in whatever form we make it, changed my view of being *good.*

There's a line in one of the Episcopal prayers that speaks of God knowing the "thoughts of our hearts." Perhaps within our soul, our essence, these thoughts are contained, and these are the thoughts we carry with us when we leave the material world behind. I know there are times the thoughts of my heart are so painful, so bitter and pitiful, that I can hardly stay in the same room with myself for an afternoon, let alone all eternity. And there are times the thoughts of my heart are joyful. Still, should I die today, I can't honestly say I'd be completely happy with the soul I have. Before I take this puppy on a cross-universe drive, it needs a good deal of tinkering and tuning.

I had a dream many years ago, but I still remember it vividly. In this dream, my boyfriend was strangling me, murdering me. My soul left my body. Suddenly light and full of joy, I began to float upwards. Then I saw my body and the man crouched over it and I remembered *the son of a bitch had killed me.* Anger suffused my spiritual being, I began to hiss and spit like an angry cat. My spirit ceased to rise, started falling back to earth, and I knew I'd lost heaven.

What if it is really sort of like that; the soul we are given soaks up whatever we choose to let it, then we must take those choices with us, *be them,* for God knows how long? When the things of the world are gone and we have only ourselves left, our essential selves, would I be made up of joy? Peace? Contentment? Or, like the me of the dream, would my hate and anger bear me back down to burn?

Religion, teachings of the spiritual, are the only guides we have on the care and nurturing of the soul. The great people of our religions, Buddha, Christ, Muhammud, Mother Teresa, Confucius, taught that we are to be *good.* From these teachings the followers codified what "good" was to mean and made laws. Some are just and sensible, some unjust and inane, but the idea is to make us better people, so that we might be able to enter heaven, that our essential essence should go on to a place of peace and joy.

Those of us who are relatively sane and haven't gone completely over to the dark side know what bliss it is to be in communion with ourselves and others, to have done the right and good thing, to have created happiness around us, to have made things a little better. We know how rotten it feels when we've hurt someone. On a visceral level we know right from wrong. Right makes us feel good. Wrong makes us feels sour and tight and defensive.

Maybe the prophets got it right, or got parts of it right. There is a consensus in many religions that we should be kind, not kill, steal, or otherwise cause harm to our neighbors and their property. Most of them suggest it's not wise to lie, commit adultery, or betray friends and family. Most tell us that it's probably not a good idea to be too slothful, lustful, greedy, or selfish, not to get too dependent on the material world for our sense of self. What if this is not because these "sins" will be recorded and some cosmic auditor will decide if there are just too many infractions to allow us to collect our heavenly reward, but because these things hurt us, corrode our essential self, damage our souls, and this damage, if unrepaired, will be something we will have to live with forever? What if the Catholics got the part right about the thought being as bad as the deed because the thought is actually caustic, blisters our souls?

Maybe this is why forgiveness plays such an important part in many teachings. He who steals my purse, steals only trash. Unless I don't forgive the thief, then he steals not only my purse but injects a bit of anger into my soul that I must carry with me. Compassion, understanding, turning the other cheek, kindness—the things we are taught are good *are* good. They are the things that cleanse the thoughts of the heart, remove the harsh corrosives of hatred, envy, bitterness, and greed.

As the priest unfolded a brochure of the charity he was pitching, I pictured life on earth. I saw it as the place we are first given this essence, the place we have to make of it what we will, refine it or defile it. I thought of the things that bring us "happiness": status, wealth, comfort, power. At death, these are stripped from us. Should my essence be focused on wealth, I'm going to lose that and be nothing. If it's dependent on power, I'll lose that, too, and be nothing. If it's full of hate, it will go on burning with hate. An eternity of hate: hell defined.

In thinking of my soul, my essence, the thoughts of my heart as real and forever, I had a different take on the teachings of the prophets. They no longer seemed to be rules that I obeyed to make life better for others (sometimes *undeserving* others) in hopes of a vague reward. But if I heed the teachings and spend my time refining my essence, perhaps when the time comes for it to leave my corporeal self I may be able to go on to an eternity of love, kindness, and joy.

I might make my eternal home a heaven.

seeking enlightenment hat by hat

I collect hats, mostly antique, mostly from the thirties and forties. I don't collect them to resell or display; I collect them to wear. This is probably a hangover from early childhood pragmatism. What's the good of a toy if one cannot play with it?

In these days of t-shirts with slogans and trousers with the crotch flapping between the knees, finding a place where one can wear a hat without engendering rude stares was a challenge. "Church," I thought. "Surely one could still wear a hat to church."

This was many years ago. Six to be exact. I'd only just begun my church-going ways and knew little about the place except that, for reasons I couldn't articulate, I wanted to be there. Little did I know that church had changed from when I saw Loretta Young attending so charmingly hatted in *The Bishop's Wife.*

Except for Easter Sunday, I am the only woman in the congregation wearing a hat. But I persevere.

There have been many Sunday mornings when the only reason I attended church was to wear a particularly wonderful hat I had come across in the dusty backroom of Grandma's attic. Usually these Sundays, the ones when sloth, busyness, or distraction made me want to stay home, were the very days I most needed to be among the community singing and praying and thinking on what really matters.

If there were no other reason for my idiosyncratic finery, that alone would be sufficient to exonerate my peculiar habit. But there are other reasons and, strangely enough, they also relate to church.

Hats, unless designed to stop the rain or protect one from the harmful rays of the sun, are totally human. Like jewelry, ties, and high-heeled shoes, we wear them to tell the world who we are, what we think about ourselves, and the people, places, and situations we are in. When I wear a hat, I feel special. Important. I am *dressed,* and I am letting the world know I am *dressed.* The vanity of this symbol radiates from myself to the event. In a hat I am *dressed* for *church,* I am giving this gathering of souls the respect of believing it to be worthy of my best, a place where dignity is of value, good manners expected. I am showing respect to my fellows: I *dressed* for you. You are important to me. I care what you think and want you to think well of me.

The last part in my addiction to hats may be the most important. Despite the outward appearance of peacockery a lady's hat evinces, when I enter a structure that we have—at least nominally—built in an attempt to honor God, a place we have, with stained glass, silver chalices, and fresh flowers, tried to show how seriously we take this need to honor Him, I am wearing a hat to cover my hair: a symbolic humbling of myself before a power I do not understand but feel to be greater than I.

Personal adornments, holidays, rituals have come in to being over the millennia to help us to differentiate the mundane from the special, the humdrum from the sacred. Somewhere along the line we have chosen to cast these differentiations aside. We no longer dress for dinner or the theater. Black-tie events are filled with people who could not take the trouble to change from their polyester pantsuits. Our Christmas trees are of plastic and we move Halloween to Friday because Wednesday is a school night.

We have changed these things not because we came up with a better way to find and honor the important events of our lives but because we have come to worship convenience above all else. We have stopped honoring our gods, our demons, our history, our dead, our aged, and our leaders because it is inconvenient to do so. It requires effort on our parts. It doesn't mesh with our too-busy schedules. In putting personal convenience above all else we have stooped to a new level of self-interest. In looking only to our own needs and comforts we are in danger of losing a sense of the wonder and grandeur of a life that is greater than making aerobics class on time or not having to bother changing for soccer as soon as service is over.

My hats, with their feathers and veils and dusty velvet, remind me that there are times in life when it is important to pay homage and respect, when it behooves me to wash my face and hands and put on my Sunday best.